JOHN SKELTON Poems sel

John Skelton (?1460–1529) live
turbulent and dangerous peri
Henry VIII), Skelton enjoyed the monarch's favour at court,
despite his outspokenness. Throughout the sixteenth century
many of Skelton's poems were printed and reprinted, including
The Bouge of Court, Philip Sparrow, Colin Clout and *The
Tunning of Elinour Rumming.*

Anthony Thwaite was born in 1930. He has been a university
teacher in Japan, Libya, Britain and the United States, was literary editor in turn of the *Listener* and the *New Statesman*, and
co-editor of *Encounter* from 1973 to 1985. His *Collected Poems*,
covering a period of fifty years, was published in 2007. As one
of Philip Larkin's literary executors, he edited Larkin's *Collected
Poems*, *Selected Letters* and *Further Requirements*. He is at present working on an edition of Larkin's letters to Monica Jones.

IN THE POET-TO-POET SERIES

W. H. AUDEN – Poems selected by John Fuller
WILLIAM BARNES – Poems selected by Andrew Motion
JOHN BERRYMAN – Poems selected by Michael Hofmann
JOHN BETJEMAN – Poems selected by Hugo Williams
ROBERT BROWNING – Poems selected by Douglas Dunn
ROBERT BURNS – Poems selected by Don Paterson
LORD BYRON – Poems selected by Paul Muldoon
THOMAS CAMPION – Poems selected by Charles Simic
JOHN CLARE – Poems selected by Paul Farley
SAMUEL TAYLOR COLERIDGE – Poems selected by James Fenton
HART CRANE – Poems selected by Maurice Riordan
EMILY DICKINSON – Poems selected by Ted Hughes
KEITH DOUGLAS – Poems selected by Ted Hughes
JOHN DRYDEN – Poems selected by Charles Tomlinson
ALLEN GINSBERG – Poems selected by Mark Ford
THOM GUNN – Poems selected by August Kleinzahler
THOMAS HARDY – Poems selected by Tom Paulin
GEORGE HERBERT – Poems selected by Jo Shapcott
GERARD MANLEY HOPKINS – Poems selected by John Stammers
A. E. HOUSMAN – Poems selected by Alan Hollinghurst
TED HUGHES – Poems selected by Simon Armitage
JOHN KEATS – Poems selected by Andrew Motion
D. H. LAWRENCE – Poems selected by Tom Paulin
ROBERT LOWELL – Poems selected by Michael Hofmann
LOUIS MACNEICE – Poems selected by Michael Longley
WILFRED OWEN – Poems selected by Jon Stallworthy
SYLVIA PLATH – Poems selected by Ted Hughes
EZRA POUND – Poems selected by Thom Gunn
WILLIAM SHAKESPEARE – Poems selected by Ted Hughes
JOHN SKELTON – Poems selected by Anthony Thwaite
WALLACE STEVENS – Poems selected by John Burnside
JONATHAN SWIFT – Poems selected by Derek Mahon
ALFRED, LORD TENNYSON – Poems selected by Mick Imlah
DYLAN THOMAS – Poems selected by Derek Mahon
WILLIAM WORDSWORTH – Poems selected by Seamus Heaney
THOMAS WYATT – Poems selected by Alice Oswald
W. B. YEATS – Poems selected by Seamus Heaney

JOHN SKELTON
Poems selected by ANTHONY THWAITE

faber and faber

First published in 2008
by Faber and Faber Limited
3 Queen Square London WC1N 3AU

Photoset by RefineCatch Ltd, Bungay, Suffolk
Printed in England by CPI Bookmarque, Croydon

A CIP record for this book
is available from the British Library

ISBN 978-0-571-23681-7

10 9 8 7 6 5 4 3 2 1

Contents

Introduction

The movement of John Skelton's reputation has been almost as much of a helter-skelter as a good deal of his own characteristic verse. He was made laureate of the universities in Oxford, Cambridge and Louvain, and *Orator Regius* at the court of Henry VIII, to whom he had been tutor in Henry's youth. Erasmus, his contemporary, called him 'the light and glory of British letters' (*'Brittanicarum literatum lumen et decus'*) – though some later commentators have pointed out that Erasmus knew no English. An Englishman, William Lily, who had himself felt the lash of Skelton's scorn, thought differently:

> May truth be said;
> Whilst thou to get the more esteem
> A Learnéd Poet fain wouldst seem,
> Skelton, thou art, let all men know it,
> Neither learned, nor a Poet.

William Winstanley, in his *Lives of the Most Famous English Poets* (1686), described him as 'the Poet Laureat in his Age, tho' now accounted only a Rhymer . . . Whoso read him, will find he hath a miserable, loose, rambling style, and galloping measure of verse.' Pope called him 'beastly Skelton'. In the later eighteenth century, Thomas Warton grudgingly allowed that 'his genius seems better suited to low burlesque, than to liberal and manly satire', and made much play with such adjectives as 'gross', 'vulgar', 'indelicate' and 'disgusting'.

It was only very slowly, following the appearance of the *Poetical Works* edited by Alexander Dyce in 1843 (until John Scattergood's marvellous 1983 *Complete English Poems* the standard edition), that Skelton began to be recognised for his special gifts. In the past eighty years he has had plenty of literary champions, from Richard Hughes and Robert Graves, both of whom edited selections of his work in the 1920s, to Edith Sitwell, W. H. Auden, George Barker, Stevie Smith, John Fuller,

Andrew Motion, Alice Oswald – disparate poets, some of whose work has been affected by Skelton's example. Modern scholarship has ferreted out his allusions, explained his feuds and quarrels, placed him crucially at the moment of clash between the medieval and renaissance cultures, and given him dignity as well as a supreme role as a satirist. He now stands almost without question as the finest English poet between Chaucer and Wyatt.

Skelton's modern reputation among other than scholars has had little to do with his learning, and has been almost wholly concerned with his energetic use of the vernacular, particularly stressed by those (such as Graves) who vaunted his 'Englishness':

> But angrily, wittily,
> Tenderly, prettily,
> Laughingly, learnedly,
> Sadly, madly,
> Helter-skelter John
> Rhymes serenely on,
> As English poets should.
> Old John, you do me good!

This hearty encomium, with its emphasis on the supposedly healthy, extrovert, life-enhancing properties of Skelton, contains an implicit criticism of morbid or artificial modes from abroad. 'Englishness' is a convenient label for many conflicting attitudes, which is why such dissimilar poets in the 1920s as Edmund Blunden and Humbert Wolfe, as well as Graves, could unite in praising this desirable quality. But it is both elusive and inaccurate, as any single descriptive word must be of such a complex person as Skelton. His 'Englishness' is in many ways a development of medieval Latin, his vocabulary a thickly spiced and eclectic brew of Latinate and literary words mixed with the demotic. The adverb 'learnedly' in Graves's catalogue must not be skated over. Caxton, praising 'Master John Skelton' in the late fifteenth century, said that he had translated Cicero's letters, the *History* of Diodorus Siculus

... and diverse other werkes oute of Latyn into Englysshe, not in rude and olde language, but in polished and ornate terms craftily, as he that hath redde Vyrgyle, Ovyde, Tully, and all the other noble poetes and oratours to me unknowen: and also hath redde the IX muses and understande theyr musicale sciences, and to whom of theym eche science is appropred. I suppose he hath dronken of Elycons well.

Clearly this is not the coarse buffoon and court-jester that stood in for Skelton during the two and a half centuries after his death when he was almost unread, and when he survived only as the saucy folk-hero of the *Merry Tales* (a collection of probably apocryphal anecdotes about Skelton, first published forty-odd years after his death). Nor is it the simple rustic prattler of the 'helter-skelter' verses praised by Graves. The real Skelton is protean, not easily summed up. He could command a dense and majestic rhetoric, as in his elegy on the Earl of Northumberland, as well as 'The Tunning of Elinour Rumming'. In *Magnificence*, he wrote the first play in English that can be read with pleasure. The lyrics in the 'Garland of Laurel' have a delicacy and subtlety that rival the songs of his younger contemporary, Wyatt. 'Speak, Parrot' is an astonishing *tour de force* of polyglot grotesqueness; but what he could do in another mood with macaronic and parody is given a quite different flavour in the tender gravity of 'Philip Sparrow'. The venom of his political satire and the exuberance of his personal abuse make him the finest master of literary invective before Pope. I have to say that I am reluctant to forgo, as John Scattergood and several other modern scholars have done, his authorship of 'Woefully Arrayed', one of the most moving devotional poems in English before Donne and Herbert; but I suppose the glancing reference to a poem of this title in the 'Garland of Laurel' is not firm enough evidence of Skelton's authorship.

In all this he was original, a pioneer. But like so many literary revolutionaries, he was also a reactionary: anti-New Learning (he resisted the spread of compulsory Greek), anti-Reformation (he detested Luther and was a virulent rooter-out of anything that might be called heresy), and perhaps his loathing of Wolsey had something to do with the notion that the Cardinal represented the rise of a new merchant-prince and merchant-cleric class. It is, in fact, the collision between the force of his conservative views and the extremity of his technical means, always exaggerating, often frenetic, that creates Skelton's peculiar energy. Paradoxically, Skelton becomes 'modern', for us, by rejecting with such pungency much that was 'modern' in his own day. It is, in various ways, a process one sees in Swift, Pope, Byron, Yeats, Eliot, Pound, Auden, Larkin.

Yet his reactionary views were not, in his poetry, put to the service of mere nostalgia, or looking back to the past for themes. He is the poet of the present moment, and his work is full of the names, trades, actions and preoccupations of England in the late fifteenth and early sixteenth centuries, the very stuff of the early Tudor age. As the French scholar Maurice Pollet has said of him: 'His poems are acts.' Whatever fancies or hyperboles or deliberate absurdities he worked into his poems, they are there with a purpose – to persuade, to preach, to sway opinions, to enlist help or rouse derision. At the centre stands no anonymous creature lost in the mists of an undifferentiated medieval past, but a man with a name, Skelton, Laureate, referring to himself by name, constantly presenting himself and determined that the voice the audience hears shall be a personal one, identifiable and idiosyncratic. Picked out by circumstance (and ambition) to be a public poet, he realised that public poetry must have an individual tang, must have a point of view and a timbre of its own, if it is not to lapse into colourless neutrality.

The language itself had to be tamed, polished, augmented, before it could become a useful weapon. As he put it in 'Philip Sparrow', through the persona of Jane Scrope:

Our natural tongue is rude,
And hard to be ennewed

With polished termes lusty;
Our language is so rusty,
So cankered, and so full
Of frowards, and so dull,
That if I would apply
To write ornately,
I wot not where to find
Terms to serve my mind.

Gower, Lydgate and Chaucer, his predecessors a century and more earlier, were to be acknowledged (and in the case of Chaucer warmly endorsed: 'His terms were not dark, But pleasant, easy, and plain; No word he wrote in vain'). But Skelton was supremely conscious of his task as a perfecter of English, which meant not only drawing on every resource of language, with all the stylistic audacity and metaphorical richness which made up late-medieval notions of 'invention', but also the skilful employment of metres and rhythms to carry the copious words. So there suddenly bubbles up the clear, piercing, almost childlike and nursery-rhyme voice of 'Philip Sparrow':

Pla ce bo!
Who is there, who?
Di le xi!
Dame Margery.
Fa, re, my, my.
Wherefore and why, why?
For the soul of Philip Sparrow
That was late slain at Carrow,
Among the Nunes Black.
For that sweet soules sake,
And for all sparrows' souls
Set in our bead-rolls,
Pater noster qui,
With an *Ave Mari,*
And with the corner of a Creed,
The more shall be your meed.

Some commentators have been tempted into ascribing Skelton's first use of this, his familiar 'Skeltonic' line, to his move to the living of Diss in the early years of the sixteenth century, as if the departure to south Norfolk marked a conscious or unconscious embracing of a bucolic style, suitable for the backwoods. But it can hardly be so. Diss at the time was a thriving wool town, not a sequestered nook. In any case there lay within easy distance both the then-great city of Norwich (though suffering at that time two devastating fires, commemorated by Skelton in Latin verses) and the estates of many county folk who would have been the new rector's social companions rather than the simple peasants with whom later sentimental critics have placed him. Skelton's choice of the rapid, dynamic, stressed short-line style (if it indeed dates from this period) must have been a literary one, and nothing to do with the move to what was after all a well-appointed benefice, from which he could still keep in close touch with the capital.

What the new line *does* reject is conventional courtliness and dignity, which is not to say that it rejects seriousness – 'Philip Sparrow', for all its parodic elements, its whimsies and its comedy, is a serious poem. The embroidered stiffness of rhyme royal, which Skelton had both enriched and loosened in 'The Bouge of Court', was discarded for what the poet himself (in *Magnificence*) later called 'bastard ryme, after the dogrell guise'. But, however deprecatory he may have been about the measure itself, it was a type of doggerel that was supremely open to verbal wit and to the profusions and decorated grace-notes of 'invention', a rhythmical staple to which any amount of ornament could be added. It was an ideal vehicle for both exuberant confusion and exaggerated mockery – the two states and attitudes in which, even in his earlier verse, Skelton felt most comfortable. The eyes that look at Elinour Rumming are bright and unwinking, observing and cataloguing with rapt intentness:

> Her eyen gowndy
> Are full unsowndy,

For they are bleared,
And she gray-haired,
Jawéd like a jetty;
A man would have pity
To see how she is gumméd,
Fingered and thumbéd,
Gently jointed,
Greased and anointed
Up to the knuckles;
The bones of her huckles
Like as they were fast with buckles
Together made fast.
Her youth is far past.

The forcefulness of this is entirely straightforward, and the clatter of rhymes, though always under control, is simply attached to the onward thrust of grotesque narrative. The 'I' who observes does little more than that. In this, Skelton has something in common with Breughel in his pictures of tavern life, peasant merrymaking and uninhibited celebration. For all the gross detail, there is very little moralising.

Such lack of commentary is rare in Skelton. Much more often he is the self-appointed scourge of corruption, of the enemies of Church and King, of the 'blother' (cant) he saw infesting all the upper reaches of society. No matter what persona he adopts – bantering bird in 'Speak, Parrot', sturdy Everyman in 'Colin Clout', or something courageously like himself in 'Why Come Ye Not to Court?' – the man is palpably there behind the poem, an amalgam of Jeremiah and Thersites. He even takes the harp of the Psalmist, in the epigraph to 'Colin Clout' – 'Who will rise up for me against the evil doers? Or who will stand up for me against the workers of iniquity? No man, Lord!'

In 'Colin Clout' he is the spokesman for 'Jack' and 'Gill', the otherwise voiceless common people, the reporter of common grievances:

> Thus I, Colin Clout,
> As I go about,
> And wandering as I walk
> I hear the people talk.

So the manner of his complaint is quite legitimately and consciously cast in the 'dogrell guise':

> For though my rhyme be raggéd,
> Tattered and jaggéd,
> Rudely rain-beaten,
> Rusty and moth-eaten,
> If ye take well therewith,
> It hath in it some pith.

In 'Speak, Parrot', the narrator is far more eccentric and subtle. The Parrot can be capricious and many-voiced, a sly mouthpiece and an all-licensed fool and jester, a polyglot surrealist, a cheeky ventriloquist's dummy, a drunken prophet, a riddling oracle. What is more, he keeps his 'little wanton eye' open as he enjoys the privilege of the most intimate chambers of the great, for he is the pet of noblemen – and, particularly, noblewomen. Thus like Philip Sparrow, he is a closet companion; but unlike Philip he has a voice:

> My lady mistress, Dame Philology,
> Gave me a gift in my nest when I lay,
> To learn all language, and it to speak aptly.

'All language', indeed: from his 'rude' beak issues Latin, Greek, French, German, Spanish, Dutch, and he can 'mew and cry' in Hebrew and Chaldean as well. He knows that *byrsa* means a thong of leather 'in Afric tongue', and he can even throw off a phrase in Welsh when the mood takes him.

Like several of Skelton's poems, 'Speak, Parrot' is a capacious hold-all, or a precarious mosaic, into which his audacious satire can be fitted to suit the moment. Wolsey and the other targets were plain for all to see, but the hand moved at such speed that their accusing eyes could never steady into focus:

Esebon, Marylebone, Whetstone next Barnet;
    A trim-tram for an horse-mill it were a nice thing.
Dainties for demoiselles, chaffer far-fet:
    Bo-ho doth bark well, but Hough-ho he ruleth the ring;
From Scarpary to Tartary renown therein doth spring,
    With 'He said', and 'We said', Ich wot now what ich wot—
Quod magnus est dominus Judas Iscariot.

Deliberately ambiguous, full of the colours and shades of allegory, it is a poem that riddles and gibes its way through dangerous political country, against the man whom Skelton saw as the evil genius manipulating the king who was once the poet's pupil. Let others in their cowardice remain silent – Parrot must speak out:

O causeless cowards, O heartless hardiness,
    O manless manhood, enfainted all with fear,
O cunning clergy, where is your readiness
    To practise or postil this process here and there?
For dread ye dare not meddle with such gear,
    Or else ye pinch courtesy, truly as I trow
Which of you first dare boldly pluck the crow.

And in the end he speaks out 'true and plain', in Parrot's great jeremiad on the condition of England in which 'a bragging butcher' could hold sway over Church and State:

So many moral matters, and so little used;
    So much new making, and so mad time spent;
So much translation into English confused;
    So much noble preaching, and so little amendment;
So much consultation, almost to none intent;
    So much provision, and so little wit at need—
Since Deucalion's flood there can no clerkes rede.

Skelton had already warned of the dangers surrounding the young King Henry, in *Magnificence*, a work that transcends the heraldic stiffness of the early Tudor morality play, and so realistic in some of its observations that it seems to have forced

Skelton into taking sanctuary of a kind more like house arrest and not far from actual imprisonment. The vices that surround Magnificence (Counterfeit Countenance, Crafty Conveyance, Cloaked Collusion and the rest) are masks for Wolsey; and though they are defeated in the end – for *Magnificence* is not a tragedy, and the King must triumph over his false friends – they have brought about a harrowing and a chastening that must have made the original audience realise that what was being revealed to them was a topical homily, not a generalised war between Vice and Virtue. The sober words spoken at the conclusion by Perseverance and Sad Circumspection are, in a sense, the mirror image of Parrot's jeremiad. The wheel of Fortune has its turns and returns: 'Today a lord, tomorrow lie in the dust.' And of course Wolsey was eventually to have the bitter taste of those words on his tongue. The poet had taken on himself the old poetic function of prophet.

Just what Skelton saw as the poet's task, together with a jaunty and amusing estimate of his own achievements and accomplishments, is set out in the 'Garland of Laurel'. In a way, the whole thing is an elaborate exercise in self-justification, and it now seems that the poem was added to and polished over a long period – from about 1495 until about 1522 – so that new works, timely new references and new obsessions were touched on. But what is likely to be most immediately attractive to the reader today is the series of interleaved lyrics, addressed to the Countess of Surrey and other aristocratic ladies, in which the tenderness of 'Philip Sparrow' is given a new courtliness and good humour. Sometimes using the dignified iambic stanza, sometimes the short line which had so much become his own, they have a playful serenity and unstriving grace that come as an appropriate coda to the barrage of contentious, vituperative verse that had occupied Skelton for so much of his career:

Merry Margaret,
As midsummer flower,
Gentle as falcon
Or hawk of the tower:

With solace and gladness,
Much mirth and no madness,
All good and no badness;
　So joyously,
　So maidenly,
　So womanly
　Her demeaning
　In every thing . . .

Indeed, until the end of his life he was a fierce and formidable combatant, buffeted in the cross-currents of the Reformation as it began its sweep through England. 'A Replication' is the final salvo from the old warrior, countering the alleged foolishness of two young men from Cambridge, Thomas Arthur and Thomas Bilney, who in the late 1520s were moving through the country spreading their reformist heresies. Arthur and Bilney recanted; and it may be hard for us now to applaud, or even to understand, the spirit of the poet who ridiculed them so contemptuously, and who in the process declared 'humble obeisance' to his arch-enemy, Wolsey. But one must make an effort of imagination to see that Skelton in this was not a time-server or trimmer but a man who passionately believed in the glorious truths of the Church and in the divinely inspired matter of true poets:

By whose inflammation
Of spiritual instigation
And divine inspiration
We are kindled in such fashion
With heate of the Holy Ghost,
Which is God of mightes most,
That he our pen doth lead,
And maketh in us such speed
That forthwith we must need
With pen and ink proceed,
Sometime for affection,
Sometime for sad direction,
Sometime for correction . . .

It is all of a piece: the man who was brave enough to assault the corrupter of his King was equally serious in his attack on those whom he thought were corrupting the Church.

But in the end we do not read Skelton for historical reasons. 'No student of the early sixteenth century', wrote C. S. Lewis, 'comes away from Skelton uncheered. He has no real predecessors and no important disciples; he stands out of the streamy historical process, an unmistakable individual, a man we have met.' There is no other early poet who speaks to us so directly, with such a passionate and pawky sense of his own nature. When we read him, almost five centuries recede and seem like yesterday:

> Go, little quaire, quickly;
>   Show them that shall you read
> How that ye are likely
>   Over all the world to spread.

ANTHONY THWAITE

Note on the Text

The texts of Skelton's poems are not straightforward or fixed. There is a widespread scatter, in British and American libraries, of both early editions and manuscripts. In 1843 the Rev. Alexander Dyce made an heroic attempt to resolve much confusing and conflicting matter. Since then, there have been many small-scale and a few large-scale ventures: selections in the 1920s by Richard Hughes and Robert Graves; a full edition, with lightly modernised spelling, by Philip Henderson in 1931, with further revisions in 1948 and 1964; an excellent selection, with full notes, by Robert S. Kinsman in 1969; and a *Complete English Poems*, edited by John Scattergood in 1983. For the scholar and specialist, Scattergood's edition is exemplary. But Penguin long ago let the book go out of print, and in any case several readers have told me they found it rather too formidable. For the present selection, I decided (after a great deal of thought and consultation) on the whole to draw on Henderson's versions, now and then adjusting his usages when I felt adjustments were improvements. About the first edition of Henderson, Robert Graves (in the *Adelphi*, III, 1931–2) was ferociously contemptuous, but I find Graves's *ad hominem* attack reflects more on Graves's irritable self-regard than on Henderson's literary sensitivity.

Biographical Note

John Skelton was born in 1460, into a family that may have come from Yorkshire. Little is known of his early days, but he seems to have begun his student life at Cambridge and to have gone on to study at Oxford, where he was crowned laureate. By 1494 he was part of the household of Henry VII, in particular acting as tutor to the Duke of York (later Henry VIII). It was here, at Eltham Palace, that he possibly became acquainted with Erasmus, who visited England in 1499. A year earlier, Skelton had taken holy orders; and when the sudden death of Prince Arthur, the heir to the throne, in 1502 caused a regrouping of the royal household, he became rector of Diss, in south Norfolk. When Henry succeeded to the throne in 1509, Skelton came back to court, where in 1512 he was appointed Orator Regius. These were the years of Wolsey's rise to power, from Archbishop of York to Lord Chancellor, and Skelton was not slow to resent Wolsey's influence on his ex-pupil. It seems that for his insolence Skelton was in sanctuary in Westminster for a time. But by the late 1520s, peace was somehow made between them; and when Skelton died, in June 1529, he was buried before the high altar of St Margaret's Church, Westminster.

JOHN SKELTON

from The Bouge of Court* (1498)

DREDE

The sail is up, Fortune ruleth our helm,
   We want no wind to pass now over all;
Favour we have tougher than any elm,
   That will abide and never from us fall.
   But under honey ofttime lieth bitter gall:
For, as methought, in our ship I did see
Full subtil persons, in number four and three.

The first was Favell, full of flattery,
   With fables false that well could feign a tale;
The second was Suspect, which that daily
   Misdeemed each man, with face deadly and pale;
   And Harvy Hafter,[1] that well could pick a male,[2]
With other four of their affinity,
Disdain, Riot, Dissimuler, Subtilty.

Fortune their friend, with whom oft she did dance;
   They could not fail, they thought, they were so sure;
And oftentimes I would myself advance
   With them to make soláce and pleasúre.
   But my disport they could not well endure:
They said they hated for to deal with Drede.
Then Favell 'gan with fair speech me to feed.

FAVELL

'No thing earthly that I wonder so sore
   As of your conning,[3] that is so excellent;
Deyntee[4] to have with us such one in store,

---

* *Bouge*, the free rations provided at Court
[1] fraudster; [2] purse; [3] learning; [4] pleasure

So virtuously that hath his dayès spent;
   Fortune to you gifts of grace hath lent:
Lo, what it is a man to have conníng!
All earthly treasure it is surmountíng.
'Ye be an apt man, as any can be found,
   To dwell with us, and serve my lady's grace;
Ye be to her, yea, worth a thousand pound!
   I heard her speak of you within short space,
   When there were divers that sore did you menace;
And, though I say it, I was myself your friend,
For here be divers to you that be unkind.

'But this one thing – ye may be sure of me;
   For, by that Lord that bought dear all mankind,
I cannot flatter, I must be plain to thee!
   An ye need ought, man, shew to me your mind,
   For ye have me whom faithful ye shall find;
Whiles I have ought, by God, thou shalt not lack,
And if need be, a bold word I dare crack!

'Nay, nay, be sure, whiles I am on your side
   Ye may not fall, trust me, ye may not fail.
Ye stand in favour, and Fortune is your guide,
   And, as she will, so shall our great ship sail:
   These lewd cockwats[1] shall nevermore prevail
Against you hardely,[2] therefore be not afraid.
Farewell till soon, but no word that I said!'

DREDE

Then thanked I him for his great gentleness.
   But, as methought, he ware on him a cloak
That linéd was with doubtful doubleness;
   Methought, of words that he had full a poke;
   His stomach stuffed oft times did reboke.

[1] rascals; [2] boldly

Suspect, methought, met him at a braid,
And I drew near to hark what they two said.

'In faith,' quod Suspect, 'spake Drede no word of me?'
   'Why? what then? wilt thou let men to speak?
He saith he cannot well accord with thee.'
   'Twyste,' quod Suspect, 'go play! him I ne reke!'
   'By Christ,' quod Favell, 'Drede is sullen freke.[1]
What, let us hold him up,[2] man, for a while?'
'Yea so,' quod Suspect, 'he may us both beguile.'

And when he came walking soberly,
   With hum and ha, and with a crooked look,
Methought his head was full of jealousy,
   His eyen rolling, his handės fast they quoke;
   And to meward the straight way he took.
'God speed, brother!' to me quod he then,
And thus to talk with me he began.

SUSPICION

'Ye remember the gentleman right now
   That communed with you, methought a pretty space?
Beware of him, for, I make God avow,
   He will beguile you and speak fair to your face.
   Ye never dwelt in such another place,
For here is none that dare well other trust—
But I would tell you a thing, an I durst!

'Spake he, i'faith, no word to you of me?
   I wot, an he did, ye would me tell.
I have a favour to you, whereof it be
   That I must shew you much of my counsél.
   But I wonder what the devil of hell
He said of me, when he with you did talk!
By mine advice use not with him to walk.

[1] man; [2] leave him alone

5

'The sovranest thing that any man may have
  Is little to say, and much to hear and see;
For, but I trusted you, so God me save,
  I wouldė nothing so plainė be:
  To you onlie, methink, I durst shrive me,
For now am I plenarly[1] disposéd
To shew you things that may not be discloséd.'

DREDE

Then I assuréd him my fidelity
  His counsel secret never to discure,
If he could find in heart to trustė me;
  Else I prayed him, with all my busy cure,[2]
  To keep it himself, for then he might be sure
That no man earthly could him betray,
Whiles of his mind it were locked with the key.

'By God,' quod he, 'this and thus it is . . .'
  And of his mind he shewed me all and some.
'Farewell,' quod he, 'we will talk more of this . . .'
  So he departed where he would be come.
  I dare not speak, I promised to be dumb.
But, as I stood musing in my mind,
Harvy Hafter came leaping, light as lynde.[3]

Upon his breast he bare a versing-box,[4]
  His throat was clear, and lustily could fayne.
Methought his gown was all furréd with fox,
  And ever he sang, '*Sith I am nothing plain . . .*'
  To keep him from picking[5] it was a great pain:
He gazed on me with his goatish beard,
When I looked on him, my purse was half afeard.

[1] fully; [2] diligence; [3] light as a lime tree, nimbly; [4] dicing-box;
[5] pocket-picking

'Sir, God you save! why look ye so sad?
    What thing is that I may do for you?
A wonder thing that ye wax not mad!
    For, an I study should as ye do now,
    My wit would waste, I make God avow!
Tell me your mind: methink ye make a verse;
I could it scan, an ye would it rehearse!
'But to the point shortly to proceed,
    Where hath your dwelling been ere ye came here?
For, as I trow, I have seen you indeed
    Ere this, when that ye made me royal cheer.
    Hold up the helm, look up, and let God steer:
I would be merry, what wind that ever blow!
Heave and ho rumbelow, row the boat, Norman, row!

'*Princes of Youth* can ye sing by rote?
    Or *Shall I sail with you* a fellowship assay?
For on the book I cannot sing a note.
    Would to God, it would please you some day
    A ballad book before me for to lay,
And learn me to sing *re mi fa sol*!
And, when I fail, bob me on the noll.

'Lo, what is to you a pleasure great
    To have that conning and ways that ye have!
By Goddès soul, I wonder how ye gate
    So great pleasúre, or who to you it gave.
    Sir, pardon me, I am an homely knave,
To be with you thus pert and thus bold:
But ye be welcome to our househóld.

'And, I dare say, there is no man therein
    But would be glad of your company.
I wist never man that so soon could win
    The favour that ye have with my ladý.
    I pray to God that it may never die.

7

It is your fortune for to have that grace—
As I be savéd, it is a wonder case!

'For, as for me, I served here many a day
    And yet unneth[1] I can have my living:
But, I require you, no wordé that I say!
    For, an I know any earthly thing
    That is again you, ye shall have weetíng.[2]
And ye be welcome, sir, so God me save!
I hope hereafter a friend of you to have.'

DREDE

With that, as he departed so from me,
    Anon there met with him, as methought,
A man, but wonderly beseen was he.
    He looked haughty; he set each man at nought;
    His gawdy garment with scornés was all wrought;
With indignatíon linéd was his hood:
He frowned, as he would swear by Cockés blood.

He bit the lip, he lookéd passing coy;
    His face was belimmed, as bees had him stung:
It was no time with him to jape nor toy.
    Envy had wasted his liver and his lung,
    Hatred by the heart so had him wrung
That he looked pale as ashes to my sight.
Disdain, I ween, this comerous crab is hight.

To Harvy Hafter then he spake of me,
    And I drew near to hark what they two said.
'Now,' quod Disdain, 'as I shall savéd be,
    I have great scorn, and am right evil apayed.'
    Then quod Harvy Hafter, 'Why art thou so dismayed?'
'By Christ,' quod he, 'for it is shame to say:
To see you Johan Dawes, that came but yesterday,

[1] scarcely; [2] you shall know about it

8

'How he is now taken in conceit,
   This Doctor Dawcock, Drede, I ween, he hight.
By Goddès bones, but if we have some slight
   It is like he will standè in our light.'
      'By God,' quod Harvy, 'and it so happen might.
Let us therefore shortly at a word
Find some means to cast him overboard.'

'By Him that me bought,' then quod Disdain,
   'I wonder sore he is in such conceit!'
'Turd!' quod Hafter, 'I will thee nothing layne,
   There must for him be laid some pretty bait;
   We twain, I trow, be not without deceit:
First pick a quarrel, and fall out with him then,
And so outface him with a card of ten.'

Forthwith he made on me a proud assault,
   With scornful look movéd all in mood;
He went about to take me in a fault;
   He frowned, he stared, he stampéd where he stood.
   I lookéd on him, I wend he had been wood.
He set the arm proudly under the side,
And in this wise he 'gan with me to chide.

DISDAIN

'Rememberest thou what thou said yesternight?
   Wilt thou abide by the words again?
By God, I have of thee now great despite!
   I shall thee angre once in every vein:
   It is great scorn to see such an hayne
As thou art, one that came but yesterday,
With us old servants suchè masters to play!

'I tell thee, I am of countenance:
   What weenest I were? I trow thou know not me!
By Goddès wounds, but for displeasance,
   Of my quarrel soon would I vengéd be.

But no force, I shall once meet with thee.
Come when it will, oppose thee I shall,
Whatsomever adventure thereof fall.

'Trowest thou, drevil I say, thou gawdy knave,
    That I have deinte to see thee cherished thus?
By Goddès side, my sword thy beard shall shave!
    Well, once thou shalt be charmed, ywis.
    Nay, straw for tales, thou shalt not rule us:
We be thy betters, and so thou shalt us take,
Or we shall thee out of thy clothès shake!'

DREDE

With that came Riot, rushing all at once,
    A rusty gallant, to-ragged and to-rent;
And on the board he whirled a pair of bones,
    Quater trey dews he clatterèd as he went.
    'Now have at all, by Saint Thomas of Kent!'
And ever he threw and cast I wote n'ere what:
His hair was growen thorough out his hat.

Then I beheld how he disguisèd was:
    His head was heavy for watching over night,
His eyen bleered, his face shone like a glass;
    His gown so short that it ne cover might
    His rump, he went so all for summer light.
His hose was garded with a list of green,
Yet at the knee they were broken, I ween.

His coat was checked with patches red and blue;
    Of Kirby Kendal was his short demi;
And aye he sang, *In faith, deacon, thou crew*;
    His elbow bare, he ware his gear so nigh;
    His nose a-dropping, his lippès were full dry;
And by his side his whinard and his pouch,
The devil might dance therein for any crowch.

Counter he could *O lux* upon a pot,
  An ostrich feather of a capon's tail
He set up freshly upon his hat aloft.
  'What revel rout!' quod he, an 'gan to rail
  How oft he had hit Jennet on the tail,
Of Phyllis fetis, and little pretty Kate,
How oft he knockéd at her clicket-gate.

What should I tell more of his ribaldry?
  I was ashaméd so to hear him prate:
He had no pleasure but in harlotry.
  'Ay,' quod he, 'in the devil's date,
  What art thou? I saw thee now but late.'
'Forsooth,' quod I, 'in this court I dwell now.'
'Welcome,' quod Riot, 'I make God avow.

RIOT

'And, sir, in faith why com'st not us among
  To make thee merry, as other fellows done?
Thou must swear and stare, man, all day long,
  And wake all night, and sleep till it be noon;
  Thou mayest not study, or muse on the moon;
This world is nothing but eat, drink, and sleep,
And thus with us good company to keep.

'Pluck up thine heart upon a merry pin,
  And let us laugh a pluck or twain at nale:
What the devil, man, mirth is here within!
  What, lo man, see here of dice a bale!
  A birdling-cast for that is in thy male!
Now have at all that lieth upon the board!
Fie on these dice, they be not worth a turd!

'Have at the hazard, or at the dozen brown,
  Or else I pass a penny to a pound!
Now, would to God, thou would lay money down!
  Lord, how that I woulde cast it full round!

Ay, in my pouch a buckle I have found,
The arms of Calais, I have no coin nor cross!
I am not happy, I run aye on the loss.

'Now run must I to the stewès side
   To weet if Malkin, my lemman, have got ought:
I let her to hire, that men may on her ride,
   Her armès easy far and near is sought:
   By Goddès side, since I her hither brought
She hath got me more money with her tail
Than hath some ship that into Bordeaux sail.

'Had I as good an horse as she is a mare,
   I durst adventure to journey thorough France;
Who rideth on her, he needeth not to care,
   For she is trussèd for to break a lance:
   It is a curtal that well can winch and prance.
To her will I now all my poverty allege,
And, till I come, have here is mine hat to pledge.'

DREDE

Gone is this knave, this ribald foul and lewd.
   He ran as fast as ever that he might.
Unthriftiness in him may well be shewed,
   For whom Tyburn groaneth both day and night.
   And, as I stood and cast aside my sight,
Disdain I saw with Dissimulation
Standing in sadè communicatíon.

But there was pointing and nodding with the head,
   And many wordès said in secret wise;
They wandered aye, and stood still in no stead:
   Methought alway Dissimuler did devise.
   Me passing sore mine heart then 'gan agrise,
I deemed and dread their talking was not good.
Anon Dissimuler came where I stood.

Then in his hood I saw there faces twain:
That one was lean and like a pinéd ghost,
That other looked as he would me have slain;
And to meward as he 'gan for to coast,
When that he was even at me almost,
I saw a knife hid in his one sleeve,
Whereon was written this word, *Mischief*.

And in his other sleeve, methought, I saw
A spoon of gold, full of honey sweet,
To feed a fool, and for to prove a daw;
And on that sleeve these wordės were writ,
A false abstract cometh from a false concrete.
His hood was syde, his cope was russet gray:
These were the words that he to me did say.

DISSIMULATION

'How do ye, master? ye look so soberly!
As I be savéd at the dreadful day,
It is a perilous vice, this envỳ.
Alas, a conning man ne dwellė may
In no place well, but foolė with him fray.
But as for that, conning hath no foe
Save him that nought can, Scripture saith so.

'I know your virtue and your literature
By that little conning that I have:
Ye be malignéd sore, I you ensure;
But ye have craft yourself alway to save.
It is great scorn to see a misproud knave
With a clerkė than conning is to prate:
Let them go louse them, in the devil's date!

'For albeit that this 'long not to me,
Yet on my back I bear such lewd dealíng:
Right now I spake with one, I trow, I see—
But what – a straw! I may not tell all thing!

By God, I say there is great heart-burníng
Between the person ye wot of and you.
Alas, I could not deal so with a Jew!

'I would each man were as plain as I!
    It is a world, I say, to hear of some:
I hate this feigning, fie upon it, fie!
    A man cannot wot where to be come.
    Ywis I could tell – but humlery, hum!
I dare not speak, we be so laid await,
For all our courte is full of deceit.

'Now by Saint Francis, that holy man and friar,
    I hate these ways again you that they take!
Were I as you, I woulde ride them full near,
    And, by my troth, but if an end they make,
    Yet will I say some wordes for your sake
That shall them angre, I hold thereon a groat:
For some shall, I ween, be hangéd by the throat!

'I have a stopping oyster in my poke,
    Trust me, an if it come to a need!
But I am loath for to raise a smoke,
    If ye could be otherwise agreed.
    And so I would it were, so God me speed,
For this may breed to a confusíon
Without God make a good conclusíon.

Nay, see where yonder standeth t'other man!
    A flattering knave and false he is, God wot;
The drevil standeth to harken, an he can.
    It were more thrift he bought him a newe coat;
    It will not be, his purse is not on float:
All that he weareth, it is borrowed ware,
His wit is thin, his hood is threadebare.

'More could I say, but what this is enow:
    Adew till soon, we shall speak more of this.

Ye must be ruled as I shall tell you how;
  Amends may be of that is now amiss.
  And I am yours, sir, so have I bliss,
In every point that I can do or say.
Give me your hand, farewell, and have good-day!'

Suddenly, as he departed me fro,
  Came pressing in one in a wonder array.
Ere I was ware, behind me he said, 'BO!'
  Then I, astoniéd of that sudden fray,
  Start all at once, I likéd nothing his play:
For, if I had not quickly fled the touch,
He had plucked out the nobles of my pouch.

He was trusséd in a garment strait:
  I have not seen such another page,
For he could well upon a casket wait;
  His hood all pouncéd and garded like a cage;
  Light lime-finger! he took none other wage.
'Hearken,' quod he, 'lo here mine hand in thine!
To us welcome thou art, by Saint Quintine.'

'But, by that Lord that is one, two, and three,
  I have an errand to round in your ear . . .
He told me so, by God, ye may trust me,
  Parde, remember when ye were there,
  There I winkéd on you – wot ye not where?
In A loco, I mean *juxta B*:
Who is him that is blind and may not see!

'But to hear the subtilty and the craft,
  As I shall tell you, if ye will hark again!
And, when I saw the whoreson would you haft,
  To hold mine hand, by God, I had great pain:

For forthwith there I had him slain,
But that I drede murder would come out:
Who dealeth with shrews hath need to look about!'

DREDE

And as he rounded thus in mine ear
   Of false collusion confetteréd by assent,
Methought I see lewd fellows here and there
   Come for to slay me of mortal intent.
   And, as they came, the shipboard fast I hent,
And thought to leap, and even with that woke,
Caught pen and ink, and wrote this little book.

I would therewith no man were miscontent,
   Beseeching you that shall it see or read
In every point to be indifferent,
   Sith all in substance of slumbering doth proceed.
   I will not say it is matter indeed,
But yet oft-time such dreams be found true.
Now construe ye what is the residue!

Philip Sparrow (1505)

Pla ce bo![1]
Who is there, who?
Di le xi![2]
Dame Margery.
Fa, re, my, my.
Wherefore and why, why?
For the soul of Philip Sparrow
That was late slain at Carrow,[3]
Among the Nunès Black.
For that sweet soulès sake,
And for all sparrows' souls
Set in our bead-rolls,
Pater noster qui,
With an *Ave Mari,*
And with the corner of a Creed,
The more shall be your meed.

When I remember again
How my Philip was slain,
Never half the pain
Was between you twain,
Pyramus and Thisbe,
As then befell to me.
I wept and I wailéd,
The tearès down hailéd,
But nothing it availéd,
To call Philip again,
Whom Gib, our cat, hath slain.

Gib, I say, our cat
Worrowéd her on that

[1] The beginning of the Office for the Dead
[2] Ps. cxvi.1: 'I am well pleased [that the Lord hath heard]'
[3] A nunnery in the suburbs of Norwich, where Jane was being educated

Which I lovéd best.
It cannot be exprest
My sorrowful heaviness,
But all without redress!
For within that stound,
Half slumbering, in a sound
I fell downè to the ground.

Unneth I cast mine eyes
Toward the cloudy skies.
But when I did behold
My sparrow dead and cold,
No crèature but that wold
Have ruéd upon me,
To behold and see
What heaviness did me pang:
Wherewith my hands I wrang,
That my sinews cracked,
As though I had been racked,
So painéd and so strainéd
That no life wellnigh remainéd.

I sighéd and I sobbed,
For that I was robbed
Of my sparrow's life.
O maiden, widow, and wife,
Of what estate ye be,
Of high or low degree,
Great sorrow then ye might see,
And learn to weep at me!
Such painès did me frete
That mine heart did beat,
My visage pale and dead,
Wan, and blue as lead:
The pangs of hateful death
Wellnigh had stopped my breath.

Heu, heu, me,[1]
That I am woe for thee!
Ad Dominum, cum tribularer, clamavi.[2]
Of God nothing else crave I
But Philip's soul to keep
From the marees deep
Of Acheronte's well,
That is a flood of hell;
And from the great Plutó,
The prince of endless woe;
And from foul Alecto,
With visage black and blo;
And from Medusa, that mare,
That like a fiend doth stare;
And from Megaera's adders
For ruZing of Philip's feathers,
And from her fiery sparklings
For burning of his wings;
And from the smokės sour
Of Proserpina's bower;
And from the denės dark
Where Cerberus doth bark,
Whom Theseus did affray,
Whom Hercules did outray,
As famous poetės say;
From that hell-hound
That lieth in chainės bound,
With ghastly headės three;
To Jupiter pray we
That Philip preservéd may be!
Amen, say ye with me!
Do mi nus,
Help now, sweet Jesus!

[1] Woe, woe is me
[2] 'In my distress, I cried unto the Lord' (Ps. cxx.1)

Levavi oculos meos in montes.[1]
Would God I had Zenophontes,
Or Socrates the wise,
To shew me their device
Moderately to take
This sorrow that I make
For Philip Sparrow's sake!
So fervently I shake,
I feel my body quake;
So urgently I am brought
Into careful thought.
Like Andromach, Hector's wife,
Was weary of her life,
When she had lost her joy,
Noble Hector of Troy;
In like manner alsó
Increaseth my deadly woe,
For my sparrow is go.

It was so pretty a fool,
It would sit on a stool,
And learnéd after my school
For to keep his cut,[2]
With 'Philip, keep your cut!'

It had a velvet cap,
And would sit upon my lap,
And seek after small wormės,
And sometime white bread-crumbės;
And many times and oft
Between my breastės soft
It wouldė lie and rest;
It was proper and prest.

Sometime he would gasp
When he saw a wasp;

[1] 'I lifted up mine eyes unto the hills' (Ps. cxxi.1)
[2] behave properly

A fly or a gnat,
He would fly at that;
And prettily he would pant
When he saw an ant.
Lord, how he would pry
After the butterfly!
Lord, how he would hop
After the gressop!
And when I said, 'Phip, Phip!'
Then he would leap and skip,
And take me by the lip.
Alas, it will me slo
That Philip is gone me fro!

    Si in i qui ta tes . . .[1]
Alas, I was evil at ease!
De pro fun dis cla ma vi,[2]
When I saw my sparrow die!

    Now, after my dome,
Dame Sulpicia at Rome,
Whose name registered was
For ever in tables of brass,
Because that she did pass
In poesy to indite
And eloquently to write,
Though she would pretend
My sparrow to commend,
I trow she could not amend
Reporting the virtues all
Of my sparrow royal.

    For it would come and go,
And fly so to and fro;
And on me it wouldè leap

---

[1] 'If [thou shouldest mark] iniquities . . .' (Ps. cxxx.3)
[2] 'Out of the depths have I cried [unto thee, O Lord]' (Ps. cxxx.1)

When I was asleep,
And his feathers shake,
Wherewith he woulde make
Me often for to wake,
And for to take him in
Upon my naked skin.
God wot, we thought no sin:
What though he crept so low?
It was no hurt, I trow
He did nothing, perde,
But sit upon my knee.
Philip, though he were nice,
In him it was no vice.
Philip might be bold
And do what he wold:
Philip would seek and take
All the fleas black
That he could there espy
With his wanton eye.

   O pe ra.[1]
La, sol, fa, fa,
Confitebor tibi, Domine, in toto corde meo![2]
Alas, I would ride and go
A thousand mile of ground!
If any such might be found
It were worth an hundred pound
Of King Croesus' gold,
Or of Attalus the old,
The riche prince of Pergame,
Whoso list the story to see.
Cadmus, that his sister sought,
An he should be bought
For gold and fee,

[1] 'The works [of the Lord are great]' (Ps. cxi.2)
[2] 'I will confess to thee, Lord, with my whole heart' (Ps. cxi.1)

He should over the sea
To weet if he could bring
Any of the offspring,
Or any of the blood.
But whoso understood
Of Medea's art,
I would I had a part
Of her crafty magíc!
My sparrow then should be quick
With a charm or twain,
And play with me again.
But all this is in vain
Thus for to complain.

   I took my sampler once
Of purpose, for the nonce,
To sew with stitches of silk
My sparrow white as milk,
That by representatíon
Of his image and fashíon
To me it might import
Some pleasure and comfórt,
For my solace and sport.
But when I was sewing his beak,
Methought my sparrow did speak,
And opened his pretty bill,
Saying, 'Maid, ye are in will
Again me for to kill,
Ye prick me in the head!'
With that my needle waxéd red,
Methought, of Philip's blood;
Mine hair right upstood,
I was in such a fray
My speech was taken away.
I cast down that there was,
And said, 'Alas, alas,

How cometh this to pass?'
My fingers, dead and cold,
Could not my sampler hold:
My needle and thread
I threw away for dread.
The best now that I may
Is for his soul to pray:
A porta inferi . . .[1]
Good Lord, have mercỳ
Upon my sparrow's soul,
Written in my bead-roll!

   Au di vi vo cem,[2]
Japhet, Ham, and Shem,
Ma gni fi cat,
Shew me the right path
To the hills of Armony,
Whereon the boards yet lie
Of your father's boat,
That was sometime afloat,
And now they lie and rot;
Let some poetès write
Deucalion's flood it hight.
But as verily as ye be
The natural sonnès three
Of Noè the patriarch,
That made that great ark,
Wherein he had apes and owls,
Beasts, birds, and fowls,
That if ye can find
Any of my sparrow's kind
(God send the soul good rest!)
I would have yet a nest

[1] 'From the gate of hell': an antiphon in the Mass for the Dead
[2] another antiphon: 'I heard a voice [from heaven say unto me, Write, Blessed are the dead]' (Rev. xiv.13)

As pretty and as prest
As my sparrow was.
But my sparrow did pass
All sparrows of the wood
That were since Noë's flood,
Was never none so good.
King Philip of Macedony
Had no such Philip as I,
No, no, sir, hardély!

That vengeance I ask and cry,
By way of exclamatíon,
On all the wholë natíon
Of cattës wild and tame:
God send them sorrow and shame!
That cat specíally
That slew so cruelly
My little pretty sparrow
That I brought up at Carrow.

O cat of carlish kind,
The fiend was in thy mind
When thou my bird untwined!
I would thou hadst been blind!
The léopards saváge,
The lions in their rage
Might catch thee in their paws,
And gnaw thee in their jaws!
The serpents of Libany
Might sting thee venomously!
The dragons with their tongues
Might poison thy liver and lungs!
The manticors of the mountaíns
Might feed them on thy brains!

Melanchaetes, that hound
That pluckéd Actaeon to the ground,

Gave him his mortal wound,
Changéd to a deer,
The story doth appear,
Was changéd to an hart:
So thou, foul cat that thou art,
The selfsame hound
Might thee confound,
That his own lordé bote,
Might bite asunder thy throat!

   Of Ind the greedy grypes
Might tear out all thy tripes!
Of Arcady the bears
Might pluck away thine ears!
The wild wolf Lycaon
Bite asunder thy backbone!
Of Etna the burning hill,
That day and night burneth still,
Set in thy tail a blaze
That all the world may gaze
And wonder upon thee,
From Ocean the great sea
Unto the Isles of Orcady,
From Tilbury Ferry
To the plain of Salísbury!
So traitorously my bird to kill
That never ought thee evil will!

   Was never bird in cage
More gentle of coráge
In doing his homáge
Unto his sovereígn.
Alas, I say again,
Death hath departed us twain!
The false cat hath thee slain:
Farewell, Philip, adew!
Our Lord, thy soul rescue!

Farewell, without restore,
Farewell, for evermore!

An it were a Jew,
It would make one rue,
To see my sorrow new.
These villainous false cats
Were made for mice and rats,
And not for birdès smale.
Alas, my face waxeth pale,
Telling this piteous tale,
How my bird so fair,
That was wont to repair,
And go in at my spair,
And creep in at my gore
Of my gown before,
Flickering with his wings!
Alas, my heart it stings,
Remembering pretty things!
Alas, mine heart it sleth,
My Philip's doleful death!
When I remember it,
How prettily it would sit,
Many times and oft,
Upon my finger aloft!
I played with him tittle-tattle,
And fed him with my spittle,
With his bill between my lips,
It was my pretty Phips!
Many a pretty kiss
Had I of his sweet muss!
And now the cause is thus,
That he is slain me fro,
To my great pain and woe.

Of fortune this the chance
Standeth on variance:

Oft time after pleasánce,
Trouble and grievánce.
No man can be sure
Alway to have pleasúre:
As well perceive ye may
How my disport and play
From me was taken away
By Gib, our cat saváge,
That in a furious rage
Caught Philip by the head
And slew him there stark dead!
    Kyrie, eleison,
    Christe, eleison,
    Kyrie, eleison!
For Philip Sparrow's soul,
Set in our bead-roll,
Let us now whisper
A *Paternoster*.

    Lauda, anima mea, Dominum![1]
To weep with me look that ye come
All manner of birdës in your kind;
See none be left behind.
To mourning lookë that ye fall
With dolorous songës funerall,
Some to sing, and some to say,
Some to weep, and some to pray,
Every birdë in his lay.
The goldfinch, the wagtail;
The jangling jay to rail,
The fleckéd pie to chatter
Of this dolorous matter;
And robin redbreast,
He shall be the priest

---

[1] 'Praise the Lord, O my soul!' (Ps. cxlvi.1)

The requiem mass to sing,
Softly warbeling,
With help of the reed sparrow,
And the chatteringė swallow,
This hearsė for to hallow;
The lark with his long toe;
The spink, and the martinet alsó;
The shoveller with his broad beak;
The dotterel, that foolish peke,
And also the mad coot,
With baldė face to toot;
The fieldfare and the snite;
The crow and the kite;
The raven, called Rolfė,
His plain-song to sol-fa;
The partridge, the quail;
The plover with us to wail;
The woodhack, that singeth 'chur'
Hoarsely, as he had the mur;
The lusty chanting nightingale;
The popinjay to tell her tale,
That toteth oft in a glass,
Shall read the Gospel at mass;
The mavis with her whistle
Shall read there the Epistle.
But with a large and a long
To keepė just plain-song,
Our chanters shall be the cuckoo,
The culver, the stockdoo.
With 'peewit' the lapwing,
The Versicles shall sing.

The bittern with his bumpė,
The crane with his trumpė,
The swan of Maeander,
The goose and the gander,

The duck and the drake,
Shall watch at this wake;
The peacock so proud,
Because his voice is loud,
And hath a glorious tail,
He shall sing the Grail;[1]
The owl, that is so foul,
Must help us to howl;
The heron so gaunt,
And the cormorant,
With the pheasant,
And the gaggling gant,
And the churlish chough;
The knot and the ruff;
The barnacle, the buzzard,
With the wild mallard;
The divendop to sleep;
The water-hen to weep;
The puffin and the teal
Money they shall deal
To poorè folk at large,
That shall be their charge;
The seamew and the titmouse;
The woodcock with the longè nose;
The throstle with her warbling;
The starling with her brabling;
The rook, with the osprey
That putteth fishes to a fray;
And the dainty curlew,
With the turtle most true.

At this *Placebo*
We may not well forgo
The countering of the coe;
The stork alsó,

[1] The *Gradual* or Antiphon

That maketh his nest
In chimneys to rest;
Within those walls
No broken galls
May there abide
Of cuckoldry side,
Or else philosophy
Maketh a great lie.

The ostrich, that will eat
An horseshoe so great,
In the stead of meat,
Such fervent heat
His stomach doth frete;
He cannot well fly,
Nor sing tunably,
Yet at a brayd
He hath well assayed
To sol-fa above E-la.
Fa, lorell, fa, fa!
Ne quando
Male cantando,[1]
The best that we can,
To make him our bell-man,
And let him ring the bells.
He can do nothing else.

   Chanticleer, our cock,
Must tell what is of the clock
By the astrology
That he hath naturally
Conceived and caught,
And was never taught
By Albumazer
The astronomer,

[1] Lest ever by singing badly

Nor by Ptolomy
Prince of astronomy,
Nor yet by Haly;
And yet he croweth daily
And nightly the tides
That no man abides,
With Partlot his hen,
Whom now and then
He plucketh by the head
When he doth her tread.

   The bird of Araby,
That potentíally
May never die,
And yet there is none
But one alone;
A phoenix it is
This hearse that must bless
With aromatic gums
That cost great sums,
The way of thurification
To make a fumigation,
Sweetė of reflarė,
And redolent of airė,
This corsė for to cense
With greatė reverence,
As patriarch or pope
In a blackė cope.
Whiles he censeth the hearse,
He shall sing the verse,
Libera me,[1]
In de la, sol, re,
Softly B molle
For my sparrow's soul.
Pliny sheweth all

[1] 'Deliver me' – the opening of the Responsory

In his *Story Natural*
What he doth find
Of the phoenix kind;
Of whose incineration
There riseth a new creation
Of the same fashíon
Without alteratíon,
Saving that oldè age
Is turnéd into corage
Of freshè youth again;
This matter true and plain,
Plain matter indeed,
Who so list to read.

    But for the eagle doth fly
Highest in the sky,
He shall be the sub-dean,
The choir to demean,
As provost principal,
To teach them their Ordinal;
Also the noble falcon,
With the ger-falcon,
The tarsel gentil,
They shall mourn soft and still
In their amice of gray;
The saker with them shall say
Dirige[1] for Philip's soul;
The goshawk shall have a roll
The choristers to control;
The lanners and the merlions
Shall stand in their mourning-gowns;
The hobby and the musket
The censers and the cross shall fet;
The kestrel in all this wark

[1] 'Direct [my steps]' – another antiphon

Shall be holy water clerk.

   And now the dark cloudy night
Chaseth away Phoebus bright,
Taking his course toward the west,
God send my sparrow's soul good rest!
Requiem aeternum dona eis, Domine![1]
Fa, fa, fa, mi, re, re,
A por ta in fe ri,
Fa, fa, fa, mi, mi.

   Credo videre bona Domini,[2]
I pray God, Philip to heaven may fly!
Domine, exaudi orationem meam![3]
To heaven he shall, from heaven he came!
   Do mi nus vo bis cum!
Of all good prayers God send him some!
       Oremus,
Deus, cui proprium est misereri et parcere,[4]
On Philip's soul have pity!
For he was a pretty cock,
And came of a gentle stock,
And wrapt in a maiden's smock,
And cherishéd full daintily,
Till cruel fate made him to die:
Alas, for doleful destiny!
But whereto should I
Longer mourn or cry?
To Jupiter I call,
Of heaven imperial,
That Philip may fly
Above the starry sky,

[1] 'Grant them eternal rest, O Lord!'
[2] 'I believe to see the goodness of the Lord' (Ps. xxvii. 13)
[3] 'Lord, hear my prayer!' (Ps. cii)
[4] 'O God, whose property it is to be merciful and to spare'

To tread the pretty wren,
That is our Lady's hen.
Amen, amen, amen!

   Yet one thing is behind,
That now cometh to mind;
An epitaph I would have
For Philippés grave:
But for I am a maid,
Timorous, half afraid,
That never yet assayed
Of Heliconés well,
Where the Muses dwell;
Though I can read and spell,
Recount, report, and tell
Of the *Tales of Canterbury*,
Some sad stories, some merry;
As Palamon and Arcet,
Duke Theseus, and Partelet;
And of the Wife of Bath,
That worketh much scath
When her tale is told
Among housewivés bold,
How she controlled
Her husbands as she wold,
And them to despise
In the homeliest wise,
Bring other wives in thought
Their husbands to set at nought.
And though that read have I
Of Gawain and Sir Guy,
And tell can a great piece
Of the Golden Fleece,
How Jason it wan,
Like a valiant man;
Of Arthur's Round Table,

With his knights commendable,
And Dame Gaynour, his queen,
Was somewhat wanton, I ween;
How Sir Lancelot de Lake
Many a spear brake
For his lady's sake;
Of Tristram, and King Mark,
And all the whole wark
Of Belle Isold his wife,
For whom was much strife;
Some say she was light,
And made her husband knight
Of the common hall,
That cuckolds men call;
And of Sir Lybius,
Named Dysconius;
Of Quater Fylz Amund,
And how they were summoned
To Rome, to Charlemagne,
Upon a great pain,
And how they rode each one
On Bayard Mountalbon;
Men see him now and then
In the forest of Ardén.
What though I can frame
The stories by name
Of Judas Maccabeus,
And of Caesar Julius;
And of the love between
Paris and Vienne;
And of the duke Hannibal,
That made the Romans all
Fordread and to quake;
How Scipion did wake
The city of Carthage,
Which by his unmerciful rage

He beat down to the ground.
And though I can expound
Of Hector of Troy,
That was all their joy,
Whom Achilles slew,
Wherefore all Troy did rue;
And of the love so hot
That made Troilus to dote
Upon fair Cresseid;
And what they wrote and said,
And of their wanton willès
Pander bare the billè[1]
From one to the other;
His master's love to further,
Sometime a precious thing,
A brooch or else a ring;
From her to him again
Sometime a pretty chain,
Or a bracelet of her hair,
Prayed Troilus for to wear
That token for her sake;
How heartily he did it take,
And much thereof did make;
And all that was in vain,
For she did but feign;
The story telleth plain,
He could not obtain,
Though his father were a king,
Yet there was a thing
That made the male to wring;[2]
She made him to sing
The song of lover's lay;
Musing night and day,

[1] i.e. *billets-doux*
[2] Wrung his withers

Mourning all alone,
Comfort had he none,
For she was quitè gone.
Thus in conclusíon,
She brought him in abusíon;
In earnest and in game
She was much to blame;
Disparaged is her fame,
And blemishéd is her name,
In manner half with shame;
Troilus alsó hath lost
On her much love and cost,
And now must kiss the post;
Pandarus, that went between,
Hath won nothing, I ween,
But light for summer green;
Yet for a special laud
He is named Troilus' bawd;
Of that name he is sure
Whilès the world shall 'dure.

Though I remember the fable
Of Penelope most stable,
To her husband most true,
Yet long-time shè ne knew
Whether he were live or dead;
Her wit stood her in stead,
That she was true and just
For any bodily lust
To Ulysses her make,
And never would him forsake.

Of Marcus Marcellus[1]
A process I could tell us;

---

[1] M. Claudius Marcellus, conqueror of Syracuse in the second Punic war, and slain by Hannibal

And of Antiochus,
And of Josephus
De Antiquitatibus;
And of Mardocheus,[1]
And of great Ahasuerus,
And of Vesca his queen,
Whom he forsook with teen,
And of Esther his other wife,
With whom he led a pleasant life;
Of King Alexander;
And of King Evander;
And of Porsena the great,
That made the Romans to sweat.

   Though I have enrolled
A thousand new and old
Of these historious tales,
To fill budgets and males
With books that I have read,
Yet I am nothing sped,
And can but little skill
Of Ovid or Virgil,
Or of Plutarch,
Or Francis Petrarch,
Alcaeus or Sappho,
Or such others poets mo,
As Linus and Homerus,
Euphorion and Theocritus,
Anacreon and Arion,
Sophocles and Philemon,
Pindarus and Simonides,
Philistion and Pherecydes;
These poets of anciente,
They are too diffuse for me:

[1] Mordecai

For, as I tofore have said,
I am but a young maid,
And cannot in effect
My style as yet direct
With English words elect.
Our natural tongue is rude,
And hard to be ennewed
With polished termės lusty;
Our language is so rusty,
So cankered, and so full
Of forwards, and so dull,
That if I would apply
To write ornately,
I wot not where to find
Terms to serve my mind.

Gower's English is old,
And of no value told;
His matter is worth gold,
And worthy to be enrolled.

In Chaucer I am sped,
His *Talės* I have read:
His matter is delectable,
Solacious, and commendable;
His English well allowed,
So as it is enprowed,
For as it is employed,
There is no English void,
At those days much commended;
And now men would have amended
His English, whereat they bark,
And mar all they wark.
Chaucer, that famous clerk,
His termės were not dark,
But pleasant, easy, and plain;
No word he wrote in vain.

    Also John Lydgate
Writeth after an higher rate;
It is diffuse to find
The sentence of his mind,
Yet writeth he in his kind,
No man that can amend
Those matters that he hath penned;
Yet some men find a faute,
And say he writeth too haut.

    Wherefore hold me excused
If I have not well perused
Mine English half abused;
Though it be refused,
In worth I shall it take,
And fewer wordès make.

    But, for my sparrow's sake,
Yet as a woman may,
My wit I shall assay
An epitaph to write
In Latin plain and light,
Whereof the elegy
Followeth by and by.

    [a brief Latin elegy follows, and concludes the poem]

The Tunning of Elinour Rumming (1517)

TELL you I chill,[1]
If that ye will
Awhile be still,
Of a comely Gill
That dwelt on a hill:
But she is not gryl,
For she is somewhat sage
And well worn in age.
For her viságe
It would assuage
A man's coráge.
    Her loathly lere
Is nothing clear,
But ugly of cheer,
Droopy and drowsy,
Scurvy and lowsy,
Her face all bowsy,
Comely crinkléd,
Woundrously wrinkléd,
Like a roast pig's ear,
Bristléd with hair.
    Her lewd lippès twain,
They slaver, men sayne,
Lik a ropy rain,
A gummy glair.
She is ugly fair.
Her nose somedele hookéd,
And camously crooked,[2]
Never stopping,
But ever dropping;

Her skin, loose and slack,
Grainéd like a sack;
With a crooked back.
 Her eyen gowndy
Are full unsowndy,
For they are bleared;
And she gray-haired,
Jawéd like a jetty;
A man would have pity
To see how she is gumméd,
Fingered and thumbéd,
Gently jointed,
Greased and annointed
Up to the knuckles;
The bones of her huckles
Like as they were with buckles
Together made fast.
Her youth is far past.
Footed like a plane,
Leggéd like a crane,
And yet she will jet
Like a jollivet,
In her furréd flocket,
And gray russet rocket,
With simper and cocket.
Her hood of Lincoln green
It had been hers, I ween,
More than forty year;
And so doth it appear,
For the green bare threadès
Look like sere weedès,
Witheréd like hay,
The wool worn away.
And yet, I darè say,
She thinketh herself gay

Upon the holy day
When she doth her array
And girdeth in her geets
Stitched and pranked with pleats;
Her kirtle Bristol-red,
With clothes upon her head
That weigh a sow of lead,
Writhen in wondrous wise
After the Saracen's guise,
With a whim-wham
Knit with a trim-tram
Upon her brain-pan;
Like an Egyptían
Cappéd about.
When she goeth out
Herself for to shew,
She driveth down the dew
With a pair of heelès
As broad as two wheelès;
She hobbles as a goose
With her blanket hose
Over the fallow;
Her shoon smeared with tallow,
Greaséd upon dirt
That baudeth her skirt.

FIT THE FIRST

And this comely dame,
I understand, her name
Is Elinour Rumming,
At home in her wonning;
And as men say
She dwelt in Surrey,
In a certain stead
Beside Leatherhead.

She is a tonnish gib,[1]
The devil and she be sib.

But to make up my tale,
She breweth nappy ale,
And maketh thereof pot-sale
To travellers, to tinkers,
To sweaters, to swinkers,
And all good ale-drinkers,
That will nothing spare
But drink till they stare
And bring themselves bare,
With '*Now away the mare!*
And let us slay care.'
As wise as an hare!

Come whoso will
To Elinour on the hill
With 'Fill the cup, fill!'
And sit there by still,
Early and late.
Thither cometh Kate,
Cisly and Sarah,
With their legs barė,
And alsó their feet
Hardely full unsweet;
With their heelės daggéd,
Their kirtles all to-jaggéd,
Their smockės all to-ragged,
With titters and tatters,
Bring dishes and platters,
With all their might running
To Elinour Rumming
To have of her tunning.

[1] a fat cat

She lendeth them on the same,
And thus beginneth the game.
  Some wenches come unlacéd,
Some housewives come unbracéd,
With their naked pappès,
That flippès and flappès,
That wiggès and waggès
Like tawny saffron baggès;
A sort of foul drabbès
All scurvy with scabbès.
Some be flybitten,
Some skewéd as a kitten;
Some with a shoe-clout
Bind their headès about;
Some have no hair-lace,
Their locks about their face,
Their tresses untrussed
All full of unlust;
Some look strawry,
Some cawry-mawry;
Full untidy teggès,
Like rotten eggès.
Such a lewd sort
To Elinour resort
From tide to tide.
Abide, abide!
And to you shall be told
How her ale is sold
To Maud and to Mold.

FIT THE SECOND

  Some have no money
That thither comè
For their ale to pay.
That is a shrewd array!
Elinour swearéd, 'Nay,

Ye shall not bear away
My ale for nought,
By Him that me bought!'
With 'Hey, dog, hey!
Have these hogs away!'
With 'Get me a staff,
The swine eat my draff!
Strike the hogs with a club,
They have drunk up my swilling-tub!'
For, be there never so much press,
These swine go to the high dais,
The sow with her pigs,
The boar his tail wrigs,
His rump alsó he frigs
Against the high bench!
With, 'Fo, there 's a stench!
Gather up, thou wench;
Seest thou not what is fall?
Take up dirt and all,
And bear out of the hall:
God give it ill-preving,
Cleanly as evil 'chieving!'

But let us turn plain,
There we left again.
For, as ill a patch as that,
The hens run in the mash-vat;
For they go to roost
Straight over the ale-joust,
And dung, when it comės,
In the ale-tunnės.
Then Elinour taketh
The mash-bowl, and shaketh
The hens' dung away,
And skimmeth it into a tray
Whereas the yeast is,
With her mangy fistės:

And sometime she blens
The dung of her hens
And the ale together,
And sayeth, 'Gossip, come hither,
This ale shall be thicker,
And flower the more quicker;
For I may tell yóu
I learned it of a Jew
When I began to brew,
And I have found it true.
Drink now while it is new:
An ye may it brook,
It shall make you look
Younger than ye be
Yearès two or three,
For ye may prove it by me.
Behold,' she said, 'and see
How bright I am of ble!
Ich am not cast away,
That can my husband say,
When we kiss and play
In lust and in likíng;
He calleth me his whiting,
His mulling and his miting,
His nobbès and his coney,
His sweeting and his honey,
With "Buss, my pretty bonny,
Thou art worth goods and money!"
Thus make I my fellow fonny,
Till that he dream and drony;
For, after all our sport,
Then will he rout and snort:
Then sweetly together we lie
As two pigs in a sty.'

To cease meseemeth best,
And of this tale to rest,

And for to leave this letter
Because it is no better,
And because it is no sweeter;
We will no further rime
Of it at this time,
But we will turnė plain
Where we left again.

Instead of coin and money
Some bringė her a coney,
And some a pot with honey,
Some a salt, and some a spoon,
Some their hose, some their shoon;
Some run a good trot
With a skillet or a pot;
Some fill their pot full
Of good Lemster wool:
An housewife of trust,
When she is athirst,
Such a web can spin,
Her thrift is full thin.

Some go straight thither,
Be it slaty or slither:
They hold the highway,
They care not what men say,
Be that as be may.
Some, loth to be espied,
Start in at the backė-side
Over the hedge and pale,
And all for the good ale.
Some runnė till they sweat,
Bring with them malt or wheat,
And Dame Elinour entreat
To birle them of the best.

Then cometh another guest:
She sweareth by the rood of rest
Her lippès are so dry
Without drink she must die,
'Therefore fill it by and by,
And have here a peck of rye.'

Anon cometh another,
As dry as the other,
And with her doth bring
Meal, salt, or other thing,
Her harvest girdle, her wedding-ring,
To pay for her scot
As cometh to her lot.
One bringeth her husband's hood
Because the ale is good;
Another brought her his cap
To offer to the ale-tap,
With flax and with tow;
And some brought sour dough
With 'Hey' and with 'Ho!
Sit we down a row,
And drink till we blow,
And pipe "Tirly Tirlow!"'

Some laid to pledge
Their hatchet and their wedge,
Their heckle and their reel,
Their rock, their spinning-wheel;
And some went so narrow
They laid to pledge their wharrow,
Their ribskin and their spindle,
Their needle and their thimble.
Here was scant thrift
When they made such shift.
Their thirst was so great
They askéd never for meat,

But 'Drink, still drink,
And let the cat wink!
Let us wash our gums
From the dry crumbs!'

FIT THE FOURTH

Some for very need
Laid down a skein of thread,
And some a skein of yarn;
Some brought from the barn
Both beanès and peas;
Small chaffer doth ease
Sometime, now and then;
Another there was that ran
With a good brass-pan,
Her colour was full wan;
She ran in all the haste,
Unbracéd and unlaced;
Tawny, swart, and sallow
Like a cake of tallow.
I swear by all hallow
It was a stale to take
The devil in a brake!
    And then came halting Joan,
And brought a gambone
Of bacon that was reasty:
But, Lord, as she was testy,
Angry as a waspy!
She began to gape and gaspy,
And bade Elinour go bet
And fill in good met;
It was dear that was far-fet.

    Another brought a spick
Of a bacon flick,
Her tongue was very quick

But she spake somewhat thick.
Her fellow did stammer and stut,
But she was a foul slut,
For her mouth foaméd
And her belly groanéd:
Joan sayn she had eaten a fiest.
'By Christ,' said she, 'thou liest,
I have as sweet a breath
As thou, with shameful death!'
    Then Elinour said, 'Ye callets,
I shall break your palates,
Without ye now cease!'
And so was made the peace.
    Then thither came drunken Alice,
And she was full of talès,
Of tidings in Walès,
And of Saint James in Galès,
And of the Portingalès,
With 'Lo, gossip, ywis,
Thus and thus it is:
There hath been great war
Between Temple Bar
And the Cross in Cheap,
And there came an heap
Of mill-stones in a rout . . .'
She speaketh thus in her snout,
Snivelling in her nose
As though she had the pose.
'Lo, here is an old tippet,
An ye will give me a sippet
Of your stale ale,
God send you good sale!'
And as she was drinking
She fell in a winking
With a barlichood,
She pissed where she stood.

Then began she to weep,
And forthwith fell asleep.
Elinour took her up
And blessed her with a cup
Of newė ale in cornės:
Alice found therein no thornės,
But supped it up at onės,
She found therein no bonės.

FIT THE FIFTH

Now in cometh another rabble:
First one with a ladle,
Another with a cradle,
And with a side-saddle:
And there began a fabble,
A clattering and a babble
Of foolish Philly
That had a foal with Willy,
With 'Jast you!' and 'Gup gilly!'
She could not lie stilly.

Then came in a jennet
And swore, 'By Saint Bennet,
I drank not this sennight
A draught to my pay!
Elinour, I thee pray,
Of thine ale let us essay,
And have here a pilch of gray:
I wear skinnės of coney,
That causeth I look so dony!'

Another then did hitch her,
And brought a pottle-pitcher,
A tunnel and a bottle,
But she had lost the stopple:
She cut off her shoe-sole,
And stoppėd therewith the hole.

Amongé all the blommer
Another brought a skommer,
A frying-pan, and a slicer:
Elinour made the pricé
For good ale each wit.

Then start in mad Kit
That had little wit:
She seeméd somedele sick
And brought a penny chick
To Dame Elinour
For a draught of liquor.

Then Margery Milkduck
Her kirtle she did uptuck
An inch above her knee,
Her legs that ye might see;
But they were sturdy and stubbéd,
Mighty pestles and clubbéd,
As fair and as white
As the foot of a kite.
She was somewhat foul,
Crooken-neckéd like an owl;
And yet she brought her fees,
A cantle of Essex cheese,
Was well a foot thick
Full of maggots quick:
It was huge and great,
And mighty strong meat
For the devil to eat:
It was tart and pungete!

Another set of sluts:
Some brought walnuts,
Some apples, some pears,
Some brought their clipping shears,
Some brought this and that,

Some brought I wot ne'er what;
Some brought their husband's hat,
Some puddings and links,
Some tripes that stinks.
  But of all this throng
One came them among,
She seeméd half a leech
And began to preach
Of the Tuesday in the week
When the mare doth kick;
Of the virtue of an unset leek,
Of her husband's breek;
With the feathers of a quail
She could to Bordeaux sail;
And with good ale barmé
She could make a charmé
To help withal a stitch:
She seemed to be a witch.
  Another brought two goslings
That were noughty frostlings;
She brought them in a wallet,
She was a comely callet:
The goslings were untied;
Elinour began to chide,
'They be wretchocks thou hast brought,
They are sheer shaking nought!'

FIT THE SIXTH

Maud Ruggy thither skippéd:
She was ugly hippéd,
And ugly thick lippéd,
Like an onion sided,
Like tan leather hided.
She had her so guided
Between the cup and the wall

That she was there withal
Into a palsy fall;
With that her head shakéd,
And her handès quakéd,
One's head would have achéd
To see her naked.
She drank so of the dreggès,
The dropsy was in her leggès;
Her face glistering like glass,
All foggy fat she was.
She had alsó the gout
In all her joints about;
Her breath was sour and stale,
And smelléd all of ale:
Such a bedfellaw
Would make one cast his craw.
But yet for all that
She drank on the mash-vat.

   There came an old ribibe:
She halted of a kibe,
And had broken her shin
At the threshold coming in,
And fell so wide open
That one might see her token,
The devil thereon be wroken!
What need all this be spoken?
She yelléd like a calf.
'Rise up, on God's half!'
Said Elinour Rumming,
'I beshrew thee for thy coming!'
And as she at her did pluck,
'Quack, quack!' said the duck
In that lampatram's lap;
With 'Fie, cover thy shap
With some flip flap!
God give it ill hap,'

Said Elinour, 'for shame!' –
Like an honest dame.
Up she start, half lame,
And scantly could go
For pain and for woe.

   In came another dant,
With a goose and a gant:
She had a wide weasant;
She was nothing pleasant,
Neckéd like an elephant;
It was a bulliphant,
A greedy cormorant.

   Another brought her garlic heads,
Another brought her beads
(Of jet or of coal)
To offer to the ale pole.
Some brought a wimble,
Some brought a thimble,
Some brought a silk lace,
Some brought a pincase,
Some her husband's gown,
Some a pillow of down,
Some of the napery
[. . .]¹
And all this shift they make
For the good ale sake.

   'A straw!' said Bely, 'stand utter,
For we have eggs and butter,
[. . .]²
And of pigeons a pair.'

   Then start forth a fizgig,
And she brought a boar pig,
The flesh thereof was rank,

¹ line missing; ² line missing

And her breath strongly stank;
Yet, ere she went, she drank,
And gat her great thank
Of Elinour for her ware
That she thither bare
To pay for her share.
Now truly, to my thinking,
This is a solemn drinking!

FIT THE SEVENTH

'Soft!' quod one hight Sybil,
'And let me with you bibble.'
She sat down in the place
With a sorry face
Whey-worméd about.
Garnishéd was her snout
With here and there a pustule
Like a scabbéd mussel.
'This ale,' said she, 'is noppy;
Let us suppé and soppy
And not spill a droppy,
For, so may I hoppy,
It cooleth well my croppy.

'Dame Elinour,' said she,
'Have here is for me—
A clout of London pins!'
And with that she begins
The pot to her pluck
And drank a 'good-luck'.
She swingéd up a quart
At once for her part:
Her paunch was so pufféd,
And so with ale stufféd,
Had she not hied apace
She had defiled the place.

Then began the sport
Among that drunken sort.
'Dame Elinour,' said they,
'Lend here a cock of hay
To make all thing clean—
Ye wot well what we mean!'

But, sir, among all
That sat in that hall
There was a prick-me-dainty
Sat like a sainty
And began to painty
As though she would fainty:
She made it as coy
As a *lege de moy*;
She was not half so wise
As she was peevish nice.
She said never a word,
But rose from the board
And calléd for our dame,
Elinour by name.
We supposéd, ywis,
That she rose to piss:
But the very ground
Was for to compound
With Elinour in the spence,
To pay for her expense.
'I have no penny nor groat
To pay,' she said, 'God wote,
For washing of my throat,
But my beads of amber
Bear them to your chamber.'
Then Elinour did them hide
Within her beddès side.

But some then sat right sad
That nothing had,

There of their own,
Neither gelt nor pawn:[1]
Such were there many
That had not a penny.
But, when they should walk,
Were fain with a chalk
To score on the balk,
Or score on the tail:
God give it ill hail!
For my fingers itch,
I have written too much
Of this mad mumming
Of Elinour Rumming.
Thus endeth the geste
Of this worthy feast.

[1] neither money nor pledge

from Magnificence (1516)

MAGNIFICENCE

Redress, in my remembrance your lesson shall rest,
 And Sad Circumspectíon I markė in my mind:
But, Perséverance, meseemeth your problem was best;
 I shall it never forget, nor leave it behind,
 But wholly to Perséverance myself I will bind,
Of that I have misdonė to make a redress,
And with Sad Circumspectíon correct my wantonness.

REDRESS

Unto this procéss briefly compiléd,
 Comprehending the world casual and transitory,
Who list to consider shall never be beguiléd,
 If it be registeréd well in memory;
 A plain example of worldly vain-glory,
How in this world there is no sickerness,
But fallible flattery enmixed with bitterness.

SAD CIRCUMSPECTION

A mirror encircléd is this interlude,
 This life inconstant for to behold and see;
Suddenly advancéd, and suddenly subdued,
 Suddenly riches, and suddenly poverty,
 Suddenly comfort, and suddenly adversity;
Suddenly thus Fortune can both smile and frown,
Suddenly set up, and suddenly cast down.

Suddenly promoted, and suddenly put back,
 Suddenly cherishéd, and suddenly cast aside,
Suddenly commended, and suddenly find a lack,
 Suddenly granted, and suddenly deniéd,

Suddenly hid, and suddenly espiéd;
Suddenly thus Fortune can both smile and frown,
Suddenly set up, and suddenly cast down.

PERSEVERANCE

This treatise, deviséd to make you disport,
   Sheweth nowadays how the world cumberéd is,
To the pith of the matter who list to resort;
   To-day it is well, to-morrow it is all amiss,
   To-day in delight, to-morrow bare of bliss,
To-day a lord, to-morrow lie in the dust:
Thus in the world there is no earthly trust.

To-day fair weather, to-morrow a stormy rage,
   To-day hot, to-morrow outragèous cold,
To-day a yeoman, to-morrow made a page,
   To-day in surety, to-morrow bought and sold,
   To-day masterfist, to-morrow he hath no hold,
To-day a man, to-morrow he lieth in the dust:
Thus in this world there is no earthly trust.

MAGNIFICENCE

This matter we have movéd, you mirthful to make,
   Pressly purposéd under pretence of play,
Showeth wisdom to them that wisdom can take,
   How suddenly worldly wealth doth decay,
   How wisdom through wantonness vanishes away,
How none estate living of himself can be sure,
For the wealth of this worldé cannot endure;

Of the terrestre richery we fall in the flood,
   Beaten with stormés of many a froward blast,
Ensorbéd with the wavés savage and wood,
   Without our ship be sure, it is likely to brast,
   Yet of magnificence oft made is the mast;

Thus none estate living of him can be sure,
For the wealth of this worldè cannot endure.

Red. Now seemeth us fitting that ye then resort
   Home to your palace with joy and royalty.
Sad Cir. Where everything is ordainéd after your noble port.
   Per. There to endure with all felicity.
   Magn. I am content, my friendès, that it so be.
Red. And ye that have heardè this disport and game,
Jesus preserve you from endless woe and shame!

Amen.

Speak, Parrot (1521)

My name is Parrot, a bird of Paradise,
　　By nature deviséd of a wonderous kind,
Daintily dieted with divers delicate spice
　　Till Euphrates, that flood, driveth me into Ind;
　　Where men of that countrỳ by fortune me find
And send me to greatė ladyės of estate:
Then Parrot must have an almond or a date.

A cage curiously carven, with a silver pin,
　　Properly painted, to be my coverture;
A mirror of glassė, that I may toot therein:
　　These, maidens full meekly with many a divers flower,
　　Freshly they dress, and makė sweet my bower,
With 'Speak, Parrot, I pray you!' full curtesly they say,
'Parrot is a goodly bird, a pretty popinjay!'

With my bekė bent, my little wanton eye,
　　My feathers fresh as is the emerald green,
About my neck a circulet like the rich rubỳ,
　　My little leggės, my feet both feat and clean,
　　I am a minion to wait upon a queen.
'My proper Parrot, my little pretty fool!'
With ladies I learn, and go with them to school.

'Ha! Ha! Ha! Parrot, yė can laugh prettily!'
　　Parrot hath not dinéd all this long day.
Like your puss-cat, Parrot can mew and cry
　　In Latin, Hebrew, Araby and Chaldy;
　　In Greekė tongue Parrot can both speak and say,
As Persius, that poet, doth report of me,
'*Quis expedivit psittaco suum chaire?*'[1]

---

[1] Who taught Parrot to say 'Hallo!' (χαῖρε)?

Doucè French of Paris Parrot can learne,
    Pronouncing my purpose after my propertỳ,
With '*Parlez bien*, Parrot, *ou parlez rien!*'
    With Dutch, with Spanish, my tongue can agree,
    In English to God Parrot can supply:[1]
'Christ save King Henry the Eighth, our royal king,
The red rose in honour to flourish and spring!

With Katherine incomparable, our royal queen alsó,
    That peerless pomegranate, Christ save her noble grace!'
Parrot *sabe hablar Castiliano*,[2]
    With *fidarsi di se stesso*[3] in Turkey and in Thrace;
    Vis consilii expers, as teacheth me Horáce,
Mole ruit sua,[4] whose dictates are pregnánt,
Soventez foys, Parrot, *en souvenante*.[5]

My lady mistress, Dame Philology,
    Gave me a giftè, in my nest when I lay,
To learn all language, and it to speak aptelỳ.
    Now *pandez mory*, wax frantic, some men say,
    Phronesis for Phrenesis may not hold her way.[6]
An almond now for Parrot, delicately drest:
In *Salve festa dies, toto* there doth best.[7]

Moderata juvant,[8] but *toto* doth exceed:
    Discretion is mother of noble virtues all.
Myden agan[9] in Greekè tongue we read.
    But reason and wit wanteth their provincial
    When wilfulness is vicar general.

---

[1] pray; [2] Can speak Castillian; [3] To trust in oneself
[4] Strength without wisdom falls by its own weight
[5] Many times within memory
[6] Understanding (or Prudence) may not avail against Frenzy
[7] On holiday it is best to go the whole hog
[8] Moderation delights us
[9] i.e. Μηδὲν αγαν – Nothing in excess

Haec res acu tangitur,[1] Parrot, *par ma foy:*
Taisez-vous, Parrot, *tenez-vous coy!*[2]

Busy, busy, busy, and business again!
   Que pensez-vous, Parrot? what meaneth this business?
Vitulus[3] in Horeb troubléd Aaron's brain,
   Melchizedek merciful made Moloch merciless:
   Too wise is no virtue, too meddling, too restléss.
In measure is treasure, *cum sensu maturato*,[4]
Ne tropo sanno, ne tropo mato.[5]

Aaron was firéd with Chaldee's fire called Ur,
   Jobab[6] was brought up in the land of Hus,
The lineage of Lot took support of Assúr,
   Jereboseth is Hebrew, who list the cause discuss—
   'Peace, Parrot, ye prate as ye were *ebrius:*[7]
Hist thee, *lieber Got von Himmelsreich, ich seg!'*[8]
In Popering grew pears when Parrot was an egg.

What is this to purpose? 'Over in a whinny Meg!'[9]
   Hob Lobin of Lowdeon[10] would hae a bit a' bread;
The gibbet of Baldock was made for Jack Leg;
   An arrow unfeatheréd and without an head,
   A bagpipe without blowing standeth in no stead:
Some run too far before, some run too far behind,
Some be too churlish, and some be too kind.

Ich dien serveth for the ostrich feather,
   Ich dien is the language of the land of Beme;[11]
In Afric tongue *byrsa* is a thong of leather;
   In Palestina there is Jerusaleme.

---

[1] i.e. this hits the nail on the head
[2] 'Shut up, Parrot, be quiet!'
[3] the calf; [4] With a mature perception;
[5] Not too sane, and not too mad;
[6] Job; [7] Drunk; [8] i.e. *sage*; [9] the beginning of a ballad;
[10] Lothian; [11] Bohemia

Colostrum[1] now for Parrot, white bread and sweet cream!
Our Thomasen she doth trip, our jennet she doth shale:
Parrot hath a blacke beard and a fair green tail.

'Morish mine own shelf!' the costermonger saith,
    '*Fate, fate, fate!*'[2] ye Irish waterlag;
In flattering fables men find but little faith,
    But *moveatur terra*, let the world wag;
    Let Sir Wrig-wrag wrestle with Sir Dalyrag;
Every man after his manner of ways,
Paub yn ei arver,[3] so the Welchman says.

Such shreddes of sentence, strewed in the shop
    Of ancíent Aristippus and such other mo,
I gader together and close in my crop,
    Of my wanton conceit, *unde depromo*
    Dilemmata docta in paedagogio
Sacro vatem,[4] whereof to you I break.
I pray you, let Parrot have liberty to speak!

But 'Ware the cat, Parrot, ware the false cat!'
    With 'Who is there – a maid? Nay, nay, I trow!'
'Ware riot, Parrot! Ware riot, ware that!'
    'Meat, meat for Parrot, meat I say, ho!'
    Thus diverse of language by learning I grow,
With 'Buss me, sweet Parrot, buss me, sweet sweet!'
To dwell among ladyes Parrot is meet.

'Parrot, Parrot, Parrot, pretty popinjay!'
    With my beak I can pick my little pretty toe;
My delight is solace, pleasure, disport, and play.
    Like a wanton, when I will, I reel to and fro.
    Parrot can say *Caesar, ave!* alsó.

---

[1] milk beestings; [2] Water, water, water!
[3] Every one in his manner
[4] Whence I produce learned arguments in the poet's sacred school

But Parrot hath no favour to Esebon.[1]
Above all other birdès, set Parrot alone.

Ulula, Esebon, for Jeremy doth weep!
    Zion is in sadness, Rachel ruely doth look;
Madionita Jethro, our Moses keepeth his sheep;
    Gideon is gone, that Zalmane undertook,
    Horeb *et* Zeb, of *Judicum* read the book.
Now Zebul, Ammon, and Abimalech – 'Hark, hark!
Parrot pretendeth to be a Bible clerk!'

O Esebon, Esebon! to thee is come again
    Sihon, the regent *Amorraeorum*,
And Og,[2] that fat hog of Bashan, doth retain
    The crafty *coistronus Cananaeorum*;
    And *asylum*, whilom *refugium miserorum*,
Non fanum, sed profanum, standeth in little stead.[3]
Ulula, Esebon, for Jephthah is stark dead!

Esebon, Marylebone, Whetstone next Barnet;
    A trim-tram for an horse-mill it were a nice thing!
Dainties for damoiselles, chaffer far-fet:[4]
    Bo-ho doth bark well, but Hough-ho he ruleth the ring;
    From Scarpary to Tartary renown therein doth spring,
With 'He said,' and 'We said,' ich wot now what ich wot[5] –
Quod magnus est dominus Judas Iscariot.[6]

Ptolemy and Haly were cunning and wise
    In the volvel,[7] in the quadrant, and in the astroloby,
To prognosticate truly the chance of Fortune's dice;

---

[1] i.e. Heshbon, capital of Sihon, King of the Amorites – that is, London
[2] Wolsey. Josephus (*Ant.* iv. v. 3) represents Og as Sihon's friend and ally
[3] Wolsey and Veysey were chiefly instrumental in abolishing the right of sanctuary
[4] far-fetched merchandise; [5] I know now what I know
[6] but mighty is lord Judas Iscariot (Wolsey)
[7] a kind of astronomical clock

Some treat of their tirykis, some of astrology,
   Some *pseudo-propheta* with chiromancy.
If Fortune be friendly, and grace be the guide,
Honour with renown will run on that side.

     Monon calon agaton,[1]
     Quod Parrato
     In Graeco.

Let Parrot, I pray you, have liberty to prate,
   For *aurea lingua Graeca* ought to be magnifiéd,
If it were conned perfitely, and after the rate,
   As *lingua Latina*, in school matter occupiéd.
   But our Greekės their Greek so well have appliéd
That they cannot say in Greek, riding by the way,
'Ho, hostler, fetch my horse a bottle of hay!'

Neither frame a syllogism in *phrisesomorum*,
   Formaliter et Graece, cum medio termino.
Our Greekės wallow in the wash-bowl *Argolicorum*;
   For though ye can tell in Greek what is *phormio*,[2]
Yet ye seek out your Greek *in Capricornio*;
For they scrape out good scripture, and set in a gall,
Ye go about to amendė, and ye mar all.

Some argue *secundum quid ad simpliciter*,
   And yet he would be reckonéd *pro Areopagita*;[3]
And some make distinctions *multiplicita*,
   Whether *ita* were before *non*, or *non* before *ita*,
   Neither wise nor well-learnéd, but like *hermaphrodita*.
Set *sophia* aside, for every Jack Raker
And every mad meddler must now be a maker.

In Academia Parrot dare no problem keep,
   For *Graece fari* so occupieth the chair
That *Latinum fari* may fall to rest and sleep,

[1] i.e. *Μόνον καλὸν ἀγαθόν* – the only beauty is goodness
[2] a straw mat; [3] as one of the senators or judges

And *syllogisari* was drownéd at Stourbridge Fair;
   Trivials and quatrivials so sore now they impair[1]
That Parrot the popinjay hath pity to behold
How the rest of good learning is roufled up and trold.[2]

Albertus de modo significandi,[3]
   And *Donatus*[4] be driven out of school;
Priseian's head broken now handy-dandy,
   And *Inter didascolos* is reckoned for a fool;
   Alexander,[5] a gander of Maeander's pool,
With *De Conciles*[6] is cast out of the gate,
And *De Rationales*[7] dare not shew his pate.

Plautus in his comedies a child shall now rehearse,
   And meddle with Quintilian in his *Declamations*,
That Petty Cato[8] can scantly construe a verse,
   With *Aveto in Graeco*,[9] and such solemn salutations,
   Can scantly the tenses of his conjugations;
Setting their minds so much on eloquence
That of their school matters lost is the whole senténce.

Now a nutmeg, a nutmeg, *cum garyophyllo*,[10]
   For Parrot to pick upon, his brainė for to stable,
Sweet cinnamon-stickės and *pleris cum musco*!
   In Paradise, that place of pleasure perduráble,
   The progeny of Parrots were fair and favouráble;
Now *in valle* Hebron Parrot is fain to feed:
Christ-Cross and Saint Nicholas, Parrot, be your good speed!

---

[1] are impaired; [2] trundled away
[3] Albertus's *Margarita Poetica*, a classical anthology (1472)
[4] a Latin grammar by Aelius Donatus
[5] a medieval grammarian; [6] the canon law(?); [7] i.e. logic
[8] *Cato Parvus* (a sort of supplement to *Cato Magnus*, i.e. *Dionysii Catonis Disticha de Moribus*) was written by Daniel Church, or Ecclesiensis, a domestic in the court of Henry II
[9] Good morning in Greek; [10] with a clove

The mirror that I toot in, *quasi diaphanum,*[1]
   Vel quasi speculum, in aenigmate,[2]
Elencticum, or else *enthymematicum,*[3]
   For logicians to look on, somewhat *sophistice*!
   Rhetoricians and orators in freshė humanity,[4]
Support Parrot, I pray you, with your suffrage ornate,
Of *confuse tantum*[5] avoiding the checkmate.

But of this supposition that callėd is art,
   Confuse distributive,[6] as Parrot hath devisėd,
Let every man after his merit take his part,
   For in this process Parrot nothing hath surmisėd,
   No matter pretended, nor nothing enterprisėd,
But that *metaphora, allegoria* with all,
Shall be his protectíon, his paves, and his wall.

For Parrot is no churlish chough, nor no fleckėd pie,
   Parrot is no pendugum, that men call a carling,
Parrot is no woodcock, nor no butterfly,
   Parrot is no stammering stare, that men call a starling.
   But Parrot is my own dear heart and my dear darling.
Melpomene, that fair maid, she burnishėd his beak:
I pray you, let Parrot have liberty to speak!

Parrot is a fair bird for a ladẏ:
   God of His goodness him framėd and wrought;
When Parrot is dead, she doth not putrefy.
   Yea, all things mortal shall turn unto nought,
   Except man's soul, that Christ so dearė bought;
That never may die, nor never die shall—
Make much of Parrot, the popinjay royall.

For that peerless Prince that Parrot did create,
   He made you of nothing by His Majesty.

[1] as though transparent; [2] or like a looking-glass, in a riddle;
[3] an elenchus [in logic] . . . an enthymeme; [4] elegant literature;
[5] so much confusion; [6] methodical confusion

Point well this probleme that Parrot doth prate,
 And remember among how Parrot and ye
 Shall leap from this life, as merry as we be:
Pomp, pride, honour, riches, and worldly lust,
Parrot saith plainly, shall turn all to dust.

  Thus Parrot doth pray you,
   With heart most tender,
  To reckon with this recueil[1] now,
   And it to remember.

Psittacus, ecce, cano; nec sunt mea carmina Phoebo
Digna scio; tamen est plena camena deo.[2]

Secundum Skeltonida famiger atum,
In Piereorum catalogo numeratum.

Itaque consolamini invicem in verbis istis.[3]

Candidi lectores, callide callete vestrum fovete Psittacum.[4]

GALATHEA

Speak, Parrot, I pray you, for Mary's sake,
What moan he made when Pamphilus lost his make.

PARROT

  My proper Bess,
  My pretty Bess,
   Turn once again to me!
  For sleepest thou, Bess,
  Or wakest thou, Bess,
   Mine heart it is with thee.

---

[1] compilation
[2] Behold Parrot, I sing; I know my songs are not worthy of Phoebus; yet the inspiration comes from the god
[3] 'Wherefore comfort one another with these words' (I Thess. iv. 18)
[4] Fair readers, shrewdly cherish your Parrot

My daisy delectable,
My primrose commendable,
My violet amiable,
My joy inexplicable,
　　Now turn again to me.

I will be firm and stable,
And to you serviceable,
And also profitable,
If ye be agreeable
　　To turn again to me,
　　　　My proper Bess.

Alas, I am disdainéd,
And as a man half maiméd,
My heart is so sore painéd!
I pray thee, Bess, unfeignéd,
　　Yet come again to me!
By love I am constrainéd
To be with you retainéd,
It will not be refrainéd:
I pray you, be reclaiméd,
　　And turn again to me,
　　　　My proper Bess.
　　　　Quoth Parrot, the popinjay royal.

Martialis cecinit carmen, fit mihi scutum: –
　Est mihi lasciva pagina, vita proba.[1]

GALATHEA

Now kus me, Parrot, kus me, kus, kus, kus!
God's blessing light on thy sweet little mus!
　　　　Vita et anima,
　　　　Zoe kai psyche.[2]

[1] cf. Martial, Ep. i. 5; [2] life and soul (Ζωὴ καὶ ψυχὴ)

Concumbunt Graece. Non est hic sermo pudicus.[1]

    Ergo   Attica dictamina
          Sunt plumbi lamina,[2]
          Vel spuria vitulamina:[3]
          Avertat haec Urania!
       Amen, Amen,
          And set too a D,
       And then it is Amend
          Our new found A.B.C.
          Cum caeteris paribus.[4]

LENVOY PRIMERE

Go, little quaire,[5] naméd the Popinjay,
   Home to resort Jeroboseth persuade;
For the cliffs of Scalop they roar wellaway,
   And the sands of Cefas begin to waste and fade,
     For replication restless that he of late there made.
Now Neptune and Aeolus are agreed of likelihood,
For Titus at Dover abideth in the road;

Lucina she wadeth among the watery floods,
   And the cocks begin to crow against the day;
Le toison de Jason[6] is lodgéd among the shrowds,
   Of Argus revengéd, recover when he may;
     Lycaon[7] of Libyk and Lydy hath caught his prey:

---

[1] They will lie together in Greek (Juvenal *Sat.* vi.191). This is not obscene talk;
[2] Greek is my shield;
[3] *Spuria vitulamina non dabunt radices altas* (Vulg., *Sap.* iv.3);
[4] with the other like things; [5] book
[6] Jason's golden fleece: a reference, perhaps, to the 400,000 crowns with which the French commissioners came to purchase Tournai, captured in 1513
[7] Who, for his impiety to Jupiter, was changed into a wolf. This probably refers to Wolsey. See later 'His wolf's head, wan, blo as lead, gapeth over the crown'

Go, little quaire, pray them that you behold
In their remembrance ye may be enrolled.

Yet some fools say that ye are furnishéd with knacks,
    That hang together as feathers in the wind;
But lewdly are they letteréd that your learning lacks,
    Barking and whining, like churlish curs of kind:
    For who looketh wisely in your workès may find
Much fruitful matter. But now, for your defence
Against all remordès, arm you with patiénce.

MONOSTICHON

Ipse sagax aequi ceu verax nuntius ito.[1]
Morda puros mal desires.[2] *Portugues.*
    Penultimo die Octobris, 33°

SECUNDE LENVOY

Pass forth, Parrot, towards some passenger,
    Require him to convey you over the saltè foam;
Addressing yourself, like a saddè messenger,
    To our sullen seignor Sadok, desire him to come home,
    Making his pilgrimage by *Nostre Dame de Crome.*
For Jerico and Jersey shall meet together as soon
As he to exploit the man out of the moon.

With porpoise and grampus he may feed him fat,
    Though he pamper not his paunchè with the Great Seal.
We have longéd and lookéd long time for that,
    Which causeth poor suitors have many a hungry meal:
    As president and regent he ruleth every deal.[3]
Now pass forth, good Parrot, our Lordè be your steed,
In this your journey to prosper and speed!

---

[1] Himself fair-minded, let him go like a truthful messenger
[2] Dyce translates: 'To bite the pure is an evil desire'
[3] This should refer to Wolsey; yet Wolsey had the Great Seal in 1515

And though some disdain you, and say how ye prate,
  And how your poemės are barren of polishéd
    eloquence,
There is none that your name will abrogate
  Than nodipolls and gramatolls of smallė intelligence;
  Too rude is their reason to reach to your senténce.
Such melancholy mastiffs and mangy cur dogs
Are meet for a swineherdė to hunt after hogs.

MONOSTICHON

Psittace perge volans, fatuorum tela retundas.[1]
Morda puros mal desires. Portugues.
In diebus Novembris,

34.

LE DEREYN LENVOY

Prepare you, Parrot, bravely your passage to take,
  Of Mercury under the trinál aspect,
And sadly salute our sullen sire Sydrake,[2]
  And show him that all the world dothė conject
  How the matters he mells in come to small effect;
For he wanteth of his wits that all would rule alone:
It is no little burden to bear a great mill-stone.

To bring all the sea into a cherrystone pit,
  To number all the starrės in the firmament,
To rule ix. realms by one man's wit,
  To such things impossible reason cannot consent.
  Much money, men say, there madly he hath spent—
Parrot, ye may prate this under protestation,
Was never such a senator since Christės incarnation!

[1] Parrot, go on flying, turn back the shafts of fatuity
[2] Wolsey (cf. *The Historie of King Boccus and Sydracke*, 1510)

Wherefore he may now come again as he went,
Non sine postica sanna,[1] as I trow,
From Calais to Dover, to Canterbury in Kent,
To make reckoning in the resset how Robin lost his bow,
To sow corn in the sea-sand, there will no crop grow.
Though he be taunted, Parrot, with tongues attainted,
Yet your problems are pregnant, and with loyalty acquainted.

MONOSTICHON

I, properans Parrote, malas sic corripe linguas.[2]
Morda puros mal desires. Portugues.
15 *Kalendis Decembris,*
34.

DISTICHON MISERABILE

Altior, heu, cedro, crudelior, heu, leopardo!
Heu, vitulus bubali fit dominus Priami![3]

TETRASTICHON

Unde species Priami est digna imperio.[4]

Non annis licet et Priamus sed honore voceris:
Dum foveas vitulum, rex, regeris, Britonum;
Rex, regeris, non ipse regis: rex inclyte, calle;
Subde tibi vitulum, ne fatuet nimium.[5]

[1] Not without a grimace behind his back
[2] Go in haste, Parrot, and thus reprove the evil tongues
[3] Higher, alas, than the cedar, more cruel, alas, than the leopard! Alas, the calf of the wild ox becomes the lord of Priam!
[4] Whence the race of Priam is worthy to rule
[5] . . . While you cherish the calf, king of Britain, you are ruled: king, you are ruled, you do not yourself rule: illustrious king, be wise, subdue the calf, lest he become too foolish

God amend all,
    That all amend may!
Amen, quoth Parrot,
    The royal popinjay.

Kalendis Decembris,

34.

LENVOY ROYAL

Go, proper Parrot, my popinjay,
    That lordės and ladies this pamphlet may behold,
With notable clerkės: supply to them, I pray,
    Your rudeness to pardon, and also that they wold
    Vouchsafe to defend you against the brawling scold
Callėd Detraction, encankerėd with envỳ,
Whose tongue is attainted with slanderous obloquy.

For truth in parable ye wantonly pronounce,
    Languages divers, yet under that doth rest
Matter more precious than the rich jacounce,[1]
    Diamondė, or ruby, or balas[2] of the best,
    Or Indy sapphire with orient pearlės drest:
Wherefore your remorders are mad, or else stark blind,
You to remord erst ere they know your mind.

DISTICHON

I, volitans, Parrote, tuam moderare Minervam:
    Vix tua percipient, qui tua teque legent.[3]

---

[1] jacinth
[2] another kind of ruby
[3] Go, flying Parrot, moderate your wit: scarce will they understand you
who read you and your writings

78

> *Psittacus hic notus seu Persius est puto notus,*
> *Nec reor est nec erit licet est erit.*

> *Maledite soit bouche malheureuse!*
>
> 34.

LECTURE DE PARROT

O my Parrot, *O unice dilecte, votorum meorum omnis lapis,*
  lapis pretiosus operimentum tuum![1]

PARROT

Sicut Aaron populumque, sic bubali vitulus, sic bubali vitulus,
  sic bubali vitulus.[2]

> Thus much Parrot hath openly expressed:
> Let see who dare make up the rest.

> *Le Popinjay s'en va complaindre:*

Helas! I lament the dull abuséd brain,
  The infatuate fantasies, the witless wilfulness
Of one and other at me that have disdain.
  Some say, they cannot my parables express,
  Some say, I rail at riot reckeless,
Some say but little, and think more in their thought,
How this process I prate of it is not all for nought.
O causeless cowards, O heartless hardiness!
  O manless manhood, enfainted all with fear!
O conning clergy, where is your readiness
  To practise or postil this process[3] here and there?

---

[1] O only loved one, the whole jewel of my prayers, a precious stone is thy
covering (cf. Ezek. xxviii. 13)
[2] As Aaron and the people, so the calf of the wild ox, etc.
[3] annotate this matter

For dread ye dare not meddle with such gere,
Or else ye pinch courtesy, truly as I trow,
Which of you first dare boldly pluck the crow.

The sky is cloudy, the coast is nothing clear;
   Titan hath trust up his tresses of fine gold;
Jupiter for Saturn dare make no royal cheer;
     Lycaon laugheth thereat, and beareth him more bold;
     Rachel, ruely ragged, she is like to catchė cold;
Moloch, that mawmet, there dare no man withstay–
The rest of suchė reckoning may make a foul fray.

       Dixit, quod Parrot, the royal popinjay.

          C'est chose malheureuse,
          Que male bouche.

PARROT

Jupiter ut nitido deus est veneratus Olympo,
   Hic coliturque deus.
Sunt data thura Jovi, rutilo solio residenti;
   Cum Jove thura capit.
Jupiter astrorum rector dominusque polorum,
   Anglica sceptra regit.[1]

GALATHEA

I compass the conveyance unto the capitall
   Of our clerk Cleros, whither, thither, and why not hither?
For pass a pace apace is gone to catch a moll,
   Over Scrapary *mala vi*, Monsire cry and slither:
   What sequel shall follow when pendugums meet together?

---

[1] As Jove is venerated in shining Olympus, he is worshipped here as a god.
Incense is given to Jove, sitting on his red-gold throne; with Jove he takes
the incense. Jove, ruler of the stars and lord of the poles, rules the English
kingdom

Speak, Parrot, my sweet bird, and ye shall have a date,
Of franticness and foolishness which is the great state?

PARROT

Difficile it is to answer this demand:
    Yet, after the sagacity of a popinjay,—
Franticness doth rule and all thing command;
    Wilfulness and brainless now rule all the ray;
    Against frantic frenzy there dare no man say nay,
For franticness and wilfulness, and brainless ensemble,
The neb of a lion they make to trete and tremble;

To jumble, to stumble, to tumble down like foolès,
    To lour, to droop, to kneel, to stoop, and to play couch quail,
To fish afore the net and to draw poolès;
    He maketh them to bear baubles, and to bear a low sail;
    He carrieth a king in his sleeve, if all the world fail;
He faceth out at a flush with 'Shew, take all!'
Of Pope Julius' cards he is chief cardinall.

He triumpheth, he trumpeth, he turned all up and down,
    With 'Skirgalliard, proud palliard, vauntperler, ye prate!'
His wolf's head, wan, blo as lead, gapeth over the crown.
    It is to fear lest he would wear the garland on his pate,
    Paregal with all princes far passing his estate.
For of our regent the regiment he hath, *ex qua vi*,
Patet per versus, quod *ex vi bolte harvi*.

Now, Galathea, let Parrot, I pray you, have his date;
    Yet dates now are dainty, and wax very scant,
For grocers were grudgéd at and groinéd at but late;
    Great raisins with reasons be now reprobitant,
    For raisins are no reasons, but reasons currant.
Run God, run Devil! yet the date of our Lord
And the date of the Devil doth shrewdly accord.

        Dixit, quod Parrot, the popinjay royal.

Now, Parrot, my sweet bird, speak out yet once again,
Set aside all sophims, and speak now true and plain.

PARROT

So many moral matters, and so little uséd;
   So much new making, and so mad time spent;
So much translatíon into English confuséd;
   So much noble preaching, and so little amendment;
   So much consultation, almost to none intent;
So much provisíon, and so little wit at need—
Since Deucalion's flood there can no clerkès rede.

So little discretion, and so much reasoníng;
   So much hardy dardy, and so little manliness;
So prodigal expense, and so shameful reckoníng;
   So gorgeous garments, and so much wretchedness;
   So much portly pride, with purses penniless;
So much spent before, and so much unpaid behind—
Since Deucalion's flood there can no clerkès find.

So much forecasting, and so far an after deal;
   So much politic prating, and so little standeth in stead;
So little secretness, and so much great counsel;
   So many bold barons, their hearts as dull as lead;
   So many noble bodies under a daw's head;
So royal a king as reigneth upon us all—
Since Deucalion's flood was never seen nor shall.

So many complaintès, and so smallè redress;
   So much calling on, and so small taking heed;
So much loss of merchandise, and so remediless;
   So little care for the common weal, and so much need;
   So much doubtful danger, and so little drede;
So much pride of prelates, so cruel and so keen—
Since Deucalion's flood, I trow, was never seen.

So many thieves hangéd, and thievės never the less;
    So much 'prisonment for matters not worth an haw;
So much papers wering for right a small excess;
    So much pillory-pageants under colour of good law;
    So much turning on the cuck-stool for every gee-gaw;
So much mockish making of statutes of array—
Since Deucalion's flood was never, I dare say.

So brainless calves' heads, so many sheepės tails;
    So bold a bragging butcher,[1] and flesh sold so dear;
So many plucked partridges, and so fattė quails;
    So mangy a mastiff cur, the great greyhound's[2] peer;
    So big a bulk of brow-antlers cabbagéd[3] that year;
So many swannės dead, and so small revél—
Since Deucalion's flood, I trow, no man can tell.

So many truces taken, and so little perfite truth;
    So much belly-joy, and so wasteful banquetíng;
So pinching and sparing, and so little profit groweth;
    So many hugy houses building, and so small householdíng;
    Such statutes upon diets, such pilling and pollíng;
So is all thing wrought wilfully withoutė reason and skill—
Since Deucalion's flood the world was never so ill.

So many vagabonds, so many beggars bold;
    So much decay of monasteries and of religious places;
So hot hatred against the Church, and charity so cold;
    So much of 'my Lord's Grace',[4] and in him no graces;
    So many hollow hearts, and so double faces;
So much sanctuary-breaking, and privilege barréd—
Since Deucalion's flood was never seen nor lyerd.

[1] Wolsey was reported to be the son of a butcher
[2] Henry VIII, in allusion to the royal arms
[3] cuckold's horns growing to a head
[4] At this time 'His Grace' was the royal style, so that it was an impertinence for Wolsey to adopt it

So much ragged right of a rammés horn;
   So rigorous ruling in a prelate specially;
So bold and so bragging, and was so basely born;
   So lordly in his looks and so disdainously;
   So fat a maggot, bred of a fleshé-fly;
Was never such a filthy Gorgon, nor such an epicure,
Since Deucalion's flood, I make thee fast and sure.

So much privy watching in cold winters' nights;
   So much searching of losels, and is himself so lewd;
So much conjurations for elfish mid-day sprites;
   So many bulls of pardon publishéd and shewed;
   So much crossing and blessing, and him all beshrewed;
Such pole-axes and pillars,[1] such mules trapt with gold—
Since Deucalion's flood in no chronicle is told.

Dixit, quod Parrot.

Crescet in immensum me vivo Psittacus iste;
Hinc mea dicetur Skeltonidis inclita fama.[2]

Quod Skelton Laureat,
Orator Regius.

34.

---

[1] A reference to the two silver pillars and four gilt pole-axes that Wolsey had carried before him in his train as he rode on his mule through the streets

[2] This Parrot will grow immensely in my lifetime; hence my glorious Skeltonian fame will be celebrated

from Colin Clout (1522)

Quis consurget mecum adversus malignantes? Aut quis stabit
mecum adversus operantes iniquitatem? Nemo, Domine![1]

   What can it avail
To drive forth a snail,
Or to make a sail
Of an herring's tail?
To rhyme or to rail,
To write or to indict,
Either for delight
Or else for despite?
Or bookès to compile
Of divers manner style,
Vice to revile
And sin to exile?
To teach or to preach,
As reason will reach?
Say this, and say that,
His head is so fat,
He wotteth never what
Nor whereof he speaketh;
He crieth and he creaketh,
He prieth and he peeketh,
He chides and he chatters,
He prates and he patters,
He clitters and he clatters,
He meddles and he smatters,
He gloses and he flatters;
Or if he speak plain,
Then he lacketh brain,

[1] 'Who will rise up with me against evil-doers? or who will stand up with
me against the workers of iniquity? No one, O Lord!' (Ps. xciv)

He is but a fool;
Let him go to school,
On a three-footed stool
That he may down sit,
For he lacketh wit!
And if that he hit
The nail on the head,
It standeth in no stead.
The Devil, they say, is dead
The Devil is dead!

　　It may well so be,
Or else they would see
Otherwise, and flee
From worldly vanity,
And foul covetousness,
And other wretchedness,
Fickle falseness,
Variableness,
With unstableness.

　　And if ye stand in doubt
Who brought this rhyme about,
My name is Colin Clout.
I purpose to shake out
All my conning bag,
Like a clerkly hag.
For though my rhyme be ragged,
Tattered and jaggéd,
Rudely rain-beaten,
Rusty and moth-eaten,
If ye take well therewith,
It hath in it some pith.
For, as far as I can see,
It is wrong with each degree:
For the temporality
Accuseth the spirituality;

The spiritual again
Doth grudge and complain
Upon the temporal men:
Thus each of other blother
The one against the other.
Alas, they make me shudder!
For in hugger-mugger
The Church is put in fault;
The prelates ben so haut,
They say, and look so high,
As though they wouldé fly
Above the starry sky.

Laymen say, indeed,
How they take no heed
Their silly sheep to feed,
But pluck away and pull
The fleeces of their wool,–
Unneth they leave a lock
Of wool among their flock!
And as for their conning,
A glumming and a mumming,
And make thereof a jape!
They gasp and they gape
All to have promotion,–
There is their whole devotion:
With money, if it will hap,
To catch the forkéd cap.[1]
Forsooth they are too lewd
To say so, all beshrewed!

What trow ye they say more
Of the bishops' lore?
How in matters they be raw,
They lumber forth the law,

[1] i.e. the mitre

To hearken Jack and Gill,
When they put up a bill,
And judge it as they will,
For other mennès skill,
Expounding out their clauses,
And leave their ownè causes.
In their provincial cure
They make but little sure,
And meddle very light
In the Church's right;
But *ire* and *venire*,
And sol-fa so a-la-mi-re,
That the praemunire
Is like to be set afire
In their jurisdictions
Through temporal aZictions.
Men say they have prescriptions
Against spiritual contradictions,
Accounting them as fictions!

   And while the heads do this,
The remnant is amiss
Of the clergy all,
Both great and small.
I wot never how they wark,
But thus the people bark,
And surely thus they say:
Bishops, if they may,
Small houses wouldè keep,
Not slumber forth and sleep,[1]
And essay to creep
Within the noble walls
Of the kingès halls,
To fat their bodies full,

[1] sleep around

Their soulės lean and dull,
And have full little care
How evil their sheep fare!

   The temporality say plain,
How bishoppės disdain
Sermons for to make,
Or suchė labour to take.
And, for to say troth,
A great part is for sloth,
But the greatest part
Is they have little art
And right slender conning
Within their headės wonning.
But this reason they take:
How they are able to make
With their gold and treasure
Clerkės out of measure,—
And yet that is a pleasure!
Howbeit some there be
(Almost two or three)
Of that dignity,
Full worshipful clerkės,
As appeareth by their workės,
Like Aaron and Ure,
The wolf from the door
To werrin and to keep
From their ghostly sheep,
And their spiritual lambės
Sequesteréd from rammės
And from the bearded goats
With their hairy coats;
Set nought by gold ne groats,—
Their names if I durst tell!

   But they are loth to mell,
And loth to hang the bell

About the cattès neck,[1]
For dread to have a check;
They are fain to play deuz deck![2]
They are made for the beck![3]
Howbeit they are good men,
Much hearted like an hen!
Their lessons forgotten they have
That Becket them gave.
Thomas *manum mittit ad fortia,*
Spernit damna, spernit opprobria,
Nulla Thomam frangit injuria![4]
But now every spiritual father,
Men say, they had rather
Spend much of their share
Than be 'cumbered with care.
Spend! nay, nay, but spare!
For let see who that dare
Shoe the mockish mare;[5]
They make her winch and kick,
But it is not worth a leek.
Boldness is to seek
The Church for to defend.
　　Take me as I intend,
For loth I am to offend
In this that I have penned:
I tell you as men say.
Amend when ye may,
For, *usque ad montem Seir,*[6]
Men say ye cannot apeir![7]
For some say ye hunt in parkès,

---

[1] loth to fix the blame; [2] a card game; [3] They are yes-men;
[4] . . . puts his hand to braver things, spurns loss, spurns dishonour,
nothing daunts Thomas;
[5] catch the offender; [6] 'Even as far as Mount Seir' (Joshua xv.10);
[7] be worse

And hawk on hobby larkės,[1]
And other wanton warkės,
When the night darkės.

    What hath laymen to do
The gray goose for to shoe?[2]
Like houndės of hell,
They cry and they yell,
How that ye sell
The grace of the Holy Ghost.
Thus they make their boast
Throughout every coast,
How some of you do eat
In Lenten season flesh meat,
Pheasants, partridge, and cranes;
Men call you, therefore, profanes.
Ye pick no shrimpės nor pranes,
Salt-fish, stock-fish, nor herring,
It is not for your wearing;
Nor in holy Lenten season
Ye will neither beans ne peason,
But ye look to be let loose
To a pig or to a goose;
Your gorgė not endewéd
Without a capon stewéd,
Or a stewéd cock,
To know what is o'clock
Under her surfléd smock,
And her wanton woodėcock!

    And how when ye give orders
In your provincial borders,
As at *Sitientes*,[3]
Some are *insuYcientes*,

---

[1] i.e. catch larks (i.e. girls) like hobbies, or hawks
[2] i.e. meddle in everything; [3] i.e. at mass – particularly on Passion Sunday

Some *parum sapientes*,
Some *nihil intelligentes*,
Some *valde negligentes*,
Some *nullum sensum habentes*,
But bestial and untaught.
But when they have once caught
Dominus vobiscum by the head[1]
Then run they in every stead,
God wot, with drunken nolls!
Yet take they cure of souls,
And wotteth never what they read,
Paternoster, Ave, nor Creed;
Construe not worth a whistle
Neither Gospel nor Epistle;
Their matins madly said,
Nothing devoutly prayed;
Their learning is so small,
Their primes and hourès[2] fall
And leap out of their lippès
Like sawdust or dry chippès!
I speak not now of all,
But the most part in general.
Of such vagabundus
Speaketh *totus mundus*;
How some sing *Laetabundus*
At every alè stake,
With, 'Welcome, hake and make!'
By the bread that God brake,
I am sorry for your sake.
I speak not of the good wife,
But of their apostles' life.[3]
Cum ipsis vel illis
Qui manent in villis

---

[1] when they have once become priests; [2] i.e. devotions and prayers
[3] i.e. of the lives of the priests' women

Est uxor vel ancilla[1]
Welcome Jack and Jilla!
My pretty Petronilla,
An you will be stilla,
You shall have your willa!
Of such Paternoster pekes
All the worldè speaks.

   In you the fault is supposéd,
For that they are not apposéd
By just examinatíon
In conning and conversatíon;
They have none instructíon
To make a true constructíon.
A priest without a letter,[2]
Without his virtue be greater,
Doubtless were much better
Upon him for to take
A mattock or a rake.
Alas, for very shame!
Some cannot decline their name,
Some can scantly read,
And yet he will not dread
For to keep a cure,
And in nothing is sure.
This *Dominus vobiscum*,
As wise as Tom-a-Thrum,
A chaplain of trust
Layeth all in the dust!

   Thus I, Colin Clout,
As I go about,
And wandering as I walk
I hear the people talk.

---

[1] with those very fellows [i.e. prelates] who stay in villas is a wife or a maid.
[2] ignorant, unlettered

Men say, for silver and gold
Mitres are bought and sold;
There shall no clergy apposè
A mitre nor a crosè,[1]
But a full purse:
A straw for God's curse!
What are they the worse?
For a simoniac
Is but a hermoniac;
And no more ye make
Of simony, men say,
But a child's play.

Over this, the foresaid lay,
Reportè how the Pope may
An holy anchor[2] call
Out of the stonè wall,
And him a bishop make,
If he on him can take
To keep so hard a rule
To ride upon a mule[3]
With goldè all betrappéd,
In purple and pall belappéd;
Some hatted and some cappéd,
Richly and warm bewrappéd,
(God wot to their great pains!)
In rochets of fine Rennes,
White as morrow's milk;
Their tabards of finè silk,
Their stirrups of mixt gold begared:
There may no cost be spared.
Their mulès gold doth eat,
Their neighbours die for meat.

---

[1] i.e. learning won't get you a bishopric or an abbey
[2] anchorite; [3] i.e. like Wolsey

    What care they though Gill sweat,
Or Jack of the Noke?
The poorė people they yoke
With summons and citatíons
And excommunicatíons,
About churches and market.
The bishop on his carpet
At home full soft doth sit.
This is a farly fit,
To hear the people jangle,
How warlike they wrangle.
Alas, why do ye not handle
And them all to-mangle?
Full falsely on you they lie,
And shamefully you ascry,
And say as untruėly
That a butterfly
(A man might say in mock)
Were the weathercock
Of the steeple of Poulės.[1]
And thus they hurt their soulės
In slandering you for truth.
Alas, it is great ruth!
Some say ye sit in thronės,
Like princes *aquilonis*,[2]
And shrine your rotten bones
With pearls and precious stones;
But how the commons groans,
And the people moans
For prestės[3] and for loans
Lent and never paid,[4]
But from day to day delayed,
The commonwealth decayed,

[1] Paul's; [2] Lucifers; [3] i.e. forced advances; [4] i.e. paid back

Men say ye are tongue-tied,
And thereof speak nothing
But dissimuling and glosing.
Wherefore men be supposing
That ye give shrewd counsél
Against the common well,
By polling and pillage
In cities and village.
By taxing and tollage,
Ye make monks to have the culerage
For[1] covering of an old cottáge,
That committed is a college
In the charter of dotage,
Tenure par service de sottage,
And not *par service de socage*,[2]
After oldè seigneurs,
And the learning of Littleton's *Tenures*.
Ye have so overthwarted,
That good lawès are subverted,
And good reason perverted.

    Religious men are fain
For to turn again
In secula seculorum,
And to forsake their quorum
And *vagabundare per forum*,[3]
And take a fine *meritorum*,
Contra regulam morum,
Aut black *monachorum*,
Aut canonicorum,
Aut Bernardinorum,

[1] i.e. for want of
[2] i.e. held for being dolts and not as payment for labours done
[3] to wander through the market-place

Aut crucifixorum,[1]
And to sing from place to place,
Like apostates.

   And the selfsame game
Begun is now with shame
Among the silly nuns.
My lady now she runs,
Dame Sibyl our abbéss,
Dame Dorothy and Lady Bess,
Dame Sarah our prioress,
Out of their cloister and choir
With an heavy cheer,
Must cast up their black veils
And set up their fuck-sails,[2]
To catch wind with their ventales–
What, Colin, there thou shales!
Yet thus with ill-hails[3]
The laity rails.

   And all the fault they lay
On your precept, and say
Ye do them wrong and no right
To put them thus to flight;
No matins at midnight,
Book and chalice gonė quite;
And pluck away the leads
Even over their heads,
And sell away their bells,

---

[1] to beg, or work for money, contrary to the rule of the order, either of the Dominicans, or of the Augustinian Canons, or of the Benedictines, or of the Cistercians
[2] Foresails – fashionable head-dresses: the implication, of course, is that they are forced to become prostitutes
[3] unhealthily

And all that they have else!
Thus the people tells,
Rails like rebèls,
Redes shrewdly and spells,
And with foundations mells,
And talks like titivels,
How ye brake the deadès wills,
Turn monasteries into water-mills;
Of an abbey ye make a grange
(Your works, they say, are strange)
So that their founders' souls
Have lost their beadèrolls,
The money for their masses
Spent among wanton lasses;
The *Diriges* are forgotten;
Their founders lie there rotten,
But where their soulès dwell,
Therewith I will not mell.
What could the Turk do more
With all his falsè lore,
Turk, Saracen, or Jew?
I report me to you,
O merciful Jesu,
Your support and rescue,
My style for to direct,
It may take some effect!
For I abhor to write
How the laity despite
You prelates, that of right
Should be lanterns of light.
Ye live, they say, in delight,
Drownéd *in deliciis*,
In gloria et divitiis,
In admirabili honore,
In gloria et splendore
Fulgurantis hastae,

Viventes parum caste.[1]
Yet sweet meat hath sour sauce:
For after *gloria, laus,*
Christ by crueltỳ
Was nailéd upon a tree;
He paid a bitter pension
For man's redemption;
He drank eisel and gall
To redeem us withal;
But sweet hippocras ye drink,
With, 'Let the cat wink!'
Ich wot what each other think.
Howbeit, *per assimile,*
Some men think that ye
Shall have penalty
For your iniquity.
Nota what I say,
And bear it well away.
If it please not theologues,
It is good for astrologues:
For Ptolemy told me
The sun sometime to be
In Ariete
Ascendant a degree,
When Scorpion descending
Was so then portending
A fatal fall of one[2]
That should sit on a throne,
And rule all things alone.
Your teeth whet on this bone
Amongst you every one,

[1] . . . in luxury, in glory and riches, in amazing state, in pomp and
magnificence with splendid possessions, living unchastely
[2] i.e. Wolsey: this passage used to be known as 'Skelton's Prophecy'

And let Colin Clout have none
Manner of cause to moan.
Lay salve to your ownė sore,
For else, as I said before,
After *gloria, laus,*
May come a sourė sauce.
Sorry therefore am I,
But truth can never lie.

With language thus polluted
Holy Church is bruted
And shamefully confuted.
My pen now will I sharp,
And wrest up my harp
With sharp twinking trebles,
Against all suchė rebels
That labour to confound
And bring the Church to the ground;
As ye may daily see
How the laity
Of one affinity
Consent and agree
Against the Church to be,
And the dignity
Of the bishops' see.

And either ye be too bad,
Or else they are mad
Of this to report.
But, under your support,
Till my dying day
I shall both write and say,
And ye shall do the same,
How they are to blame
You thus to defame.
For it maketh me sad
How that the people are glad

The Church to deprave;
And some there are that rave,
Presuming on their wit,
When there is never a whit
To maintain arguments
Against the sacraments.

Some make epilogatíon.
Of high predestinatíon;
And of recidivatíon
They make interpretatíon
Of an awkward fashíon;
And of the prescience
Of divine essence;
And what hypostasis
Of Christ's manhood is.
Such logic men will chop,
And in their fury hop,
When the good ale sop
Doth dance in their foretop!
Bothė women and men,
Such ye may well know and ken.
That against priesthood
Their malice spread abroad,
Railing heinously
And disdainously
Of priestly dignities,
With their malignities.

And some have a smack
Of Luther's sack,
And a burning spark
Of Luther's wark,
And are somewhat suspect
In Luther's sect;
And some of them bark,
Clatter and carp

Of that heresiarch
Called Wicliffista,
The devilish dogmatista;
And some be Hussians,
And some be Arians,
And some be Pelagians,
And make much variance
Between the clergy
And the temporalty,
How the Church hath too mickle,
And they have too little,
And bring in materialities
And qualified qualities
Of pluralities,
Of trialities,[1]
And of tot quots[2]
They commune like sots,
As cometh to their lots;
Of prebendaries and deans,
How some of them gleans
And gathereth up the store
For to catch more and more;
Of parsons and vicaries
They make many outcries—
They cannot keep their wives
From them for their lives!
And thus the losels strives,
And lewdly says, by Christ,
Against the silly priest.
Alas, and wellaway,
What ails them thus to say?
They might be better adviséd
Than to be so disguiséd![3]

[1] triple benefices; [2] dispensations; [3] behave so badly

But they have enterpриséd,
And shamefully surmiséd,
How prelacy is sold and bought,
And come up of nought;
And where the prelates be
Come of low degree,
And set in majesty
And spiritual dignity,
Farewell benignity,
Farewell simplicity,
Farewell humility,
Farewell good charity!

   Ye are so puffed with pride,[1]
That no man may abide
Your high and lordly looks:
Ye cast up then your books,
And virtue is forgotten;
For then ye will be wroken
Of every light quarrél,
And call a lord a javel,
A knight a knave ye make;
Ye boast, ye face, ye crake,
And upon you ye take
To rule both king and kaiser;
An if ye may have leisure,
Ye will bring all to nought,
And that is all your thought!
For the lordès temporal,
Their rule is very small,
Almost nothing at all.
Men say how ye appal
The noble blood royall.
In earnest and in game,

---

[1] Wolsey

Ye are the less to blame,
For lords of noble blood,
If they well understood
How conning might them advance,
They would pipe you another dance.
But noblemen born
To learn they have scorn,
But hunt and blow an horn,
Leap over lakes and dykes,
Set nothing by politics.
Therefore ye keep them base,
And mock them to their face.
This is a piteous case!
To you that be on the wheel[1]
Great lords must crouch and kneel,
And break their hose at the knee,
As daily men may see,
And to remembrance call.
Fortune so turneth the ball
And ruleth so over all,
That honour hath a great fall.

    Shall I tell you more? yea, shall.
I am loth to tell all;
But the commonalty you call[2]
Idols of Babylon,
De Terra Zabulon,
De Terra Neptalim;
For ye love to go trim,
Brought up of poor estate,
With pride inordinate,
Suddenly upstart
From the dung-cart,
The mattock and the shule,

To reign and to rule;
And have no grace to think
How ye were wont to drink
Of a leather bottle
With a knavish stopple,
When mammocks was your meat,
With mouldy bread to eat;
Ye could none other get
To chew and to gnaw,
To fill therewith your maw;
Lodging in fairè straw,
Couching your drowsy heads
Sometime in lousy beds.
Alas, this is out of mind!
Ye grow now out of kind.
Many one ye have untwined,
And made the commons blind.
But *qui se existimat stare*,[1]
Let him well bewarè
Lest that his foot slip,
And have such a trip,
And fall in such decay,
That all the world may say,
'Come down, in the devil way!'

Yet, over all that,
Of bishops they chat,
That though ye round your hair
An inch above your ear,
And have *aures patentes*[2]
And *parum intendentes*,[3]
And your tonsures be croppéd,
Your ears they be stoppéd!

---

[1] 'Who thinketh he standeth . . .' (I Cor. x.12); [2] open ears
[3] too little hearing

For Master *Adulator*,[1]
And Doctor *Assentator*,[2]
And *Blandior blandiris*,[3]
With *Mentior mentiris*,[4]
They follow your desirės,
And so they blear your eye,[5]
That ye cannot espy
How the male doth wry.[6]

   Alas, for God's will,
Why sit ye, prelates, still
And suffer all this ill?
Ye bishops of estates[7]
Should open the broad gates
Of your spiritual charge,
And come forth at large,
Like lanterns of light,
In the people's sight,
In pulpits authentic,
For the weal public
Of priesthood in this case;
And always to chase
Such manner of schismatics
And half heretics,
That would intoxicate,
That would coinquinate,
That would contaminate,
And that would violate,
And that would derogate,
And that would abrogate
The Church's high estates,[8]
After this manner rates,—
The which should be

---

[1] sycophant; [2] yes-man; [3] I flatter, you flatter; [4] I lie, you lie;
[5] do you in the eye; [6] how everything goes awry; [7] of high rank;
[8] dignitaries

Both frank and free,
And have their liberty,
As of antiquity
It was ratified,
And also gratified,
By holy synodals
And bulls papals,
As it is *res certa*
Contained in *Magna Charta*.

[. . .]

But now my mind ye understand,
For they must take in hand
To preach, and to withstand
All manner of objections;
For bishops have protections,
They say, to do corrections,
But they have no affections
To take the said directions.
In such manner of cases,
Men say, they bear no faces
To occupy such places,
To sow the seed of graces:
Their heartès are so fainted,
And they be so attainted
With covetise and ambition,
And other superstition,
That they be deaf and dumb,
And play silence and glum,
Can say nothing but 'Mum!'

They occupy them so
With singing *Placebo*,
They will no farther go:
They had liefer to please,
And take their worldly ease,

Than to take on hand
Worshipfully to withstand
Such temporal war and bate
As now is made of late
Against Holy Church estate,
Or to maintain good quarrels.
The lay men call them barrels
Full of gluttony
And of hypocrisy,
That counterfeits and paints
As they were very saints.
In matters that them like
They shew them politic,
Pretending gravity
And signiority,
With all solemnity,
For their indemnity!
For they will have no loss
Of a penny nor of a cross
Of their predial lands,
That cometh to their hands,
And as far as they dare set,
All is fish that cometh to net.
Building royally
Their mansions curiously,
With turrets and with towers,
With hallès and with bowers,
Stretching to the stars,
With glass windows and bars;
Hanging about the wallès
Cloths of gold and pallès,
Arras of rich array,
Fresh as flowers in May;
With dame Diana naked;
How lusty Venus quakéd,
And how Cupid shakéd

His dart, and bent his bow
For to shoot a crow
At her tirly tirlow;
And how Paris of Troy
Dancéd a lege de moy,
Made lusty sport and joy
With dame Helen the queen;
With such stories bydene
With Triumphs of Cæsar,
And of Pompeius' war,
Of renown and of fame,
By them to get a name.
Now all the worldé stares,
How they ride in goodly chairs,
Conveyéd by elephants,
With laureate garlants,
And by unicornés
With their seemly hornés;
Upon these beastés riding,
Naked boyés striding,
With wanton wenches winking.
Now truly, to my thinking,
That is a speculatíon
And a meet meditatíon
For prelates of estate,
Their corage to abate
From worldly wantonness,
Their chambers thus to dress
With such parfitness
And all such holiness!
Howbeit they let down fall
Their churches cathedrall.

  Squire, knight, and lord,
Thus the Church remord;
With all temporal people

They run against the steeple,
Thus talking and telling
How some of you are melling,
Yet soft and fair for swelling—
Beware of a quean's yelling.
It is a busy thing
For one man to rule a king
Alone and make reckoning,
To govern over all
And rule a realm royall
By one man's very wit.
Fortune may chance to flit,
And when he weneth to sit,
Yet may he miss the cushion.
For I rede a preposition—
Cum regibus amicare,
Et omnibus dominari,
Et supra te pravare.[1]
Wherefore he hath good ure
That can himself assure
How fortune will endure.
Then let reason you support,
For the commonalty doth report
That they have great wonder
That ye keep them so under;
Yet they marvel so much less,
For ye play so at the chess,
As they suppose and guess,
That some of you but late
Hath playéd so checkmate
With lords of great estate,
After such a rate,
That they shall mell nor make,
Nor upon them take,

[1] To be friendly with kings, and all things to rule, and to overleap thyself

For king's nor kaiser's sake,
But at the pleasure of one
That ruleth the roast alone.

Helas, I say, helas!
How may this come to pass,
That a man shall hear a mass,
And not so hardy on his head
To look on God in form of bread,
But that the parish clerk
Thereupon must hark,
And grant him at his asking
For to see the sacring?

And how may this accord,
No man to our sovereign lord
So hardy to make suit,
Nor yet to execute
His commandment,
Without the assent
Of our president,
Nor to express to his person,
Without your consentation
Grant him his licence
To press to his presence,
Nor to speak to him secretly,
Openly nor privily,
Without this president be by,
Or else his substitute
Whom he will depute?
Neither earl ne duke
Permitted? By saint Luke,
And by sweet saint Mark,
This is a wondrous wark!
That the people talkè this,
Somewhat there is amiss.
The Devil cannot stop their mouths,

But they will talk of such uncouths,
All that ever they ken
Against all spiritual men!

   Whether it be wrong or right,
Or else for despite,
Or however it hap,
Their tongues thus do clap,
And through such detraction
They put you to your action;
And whether they say truly
As they may abide thereby,
Or else that they do lie,
Ye know better than I!
But now *debetis scire*,
And groundly *audire*,
In your *convenire*,
Of this praemunire,
Or else in the mirė
They say they will you cast.
Therefore stand sure and fast!

   Stand sure, and take good footing,
And let be all your mooting,
Your gasping and your tooting,
And your partíal promoting
Of those that stand in your grace.
But oldė servants ye chase,
And put them out of their place.
Make ye no murmuration,
Though I write after this fashion;
Though I, Colin Clout,
Among the wholė rout
Of you that clerkės be,
Take now upon me
Thus copiously to write,
I do it for no despite.

Wherefore take no disdain
At my style rude and plain;
For I rebuke no man
That virtuous is: why then
Wreak ye your anger on me?
For those that virtuous be
Have no cause to say
That I speak out of the way.

   Of no good bishop speak I,
Nor good priest I ascry,
Good friar, nor good chanon,
Good nunnė, nor good canon,
Good monkė, nor good clerk,
Nor yet of no good work.
But my recounting is
Of them that do amiss,
In speaking and rebelling,
In hindering and disavailing
Holy Church, our mother,
One against another.
To use such despiting
Is all my wholė writing;
To hinder no man,
As near as I can,
For no man have I naméd:
Wherefore should I be blaméd?
Ye ought to be ashaméd,
Against me to be graméd,
And can tell no cause why,
But that I write truly!

   Then if any there be
Of high or low degree
Of the spirituality,
Or of the temporality,
That doth think or ween

That his conscience be not clean,
And feeleth himself sick,
Or touchéd on the quick,
Such grace God them send
Themselfè to amend,—
For I will not pretend
Any man to offend.

   Wherefore, as thinketh me,
Great idiots they be,
And little grace they have,
This treatise to deprave;
Nor will hear no preaching,
Nor no virtuous teaching,
Nor will have no resting
Of any virtuous writing;
Will know none intelligence
To reform their negligence,
But live still out of fashíon,
To their own damnatíon.
To do shame they have no shame,
But they would no man should them blame!
They have an evil name,
But yet they will occupy the same!

   With them the word of God
Is counted for no rod;
They count it for a railing,
That nothing is availing.
The preachers with evil hailing:
'Shall they daunt us prelates,
That be their primates?
Not so hardy on their pates!
Hark, how the losel prates,
With a wide wesaunt!
Avaunt, sir Guy of Gaunt!
Avaunt, lewd priest, avaunt!

Avaunt, sir doctor Devias!
Prate of thy matins and thy mass,
And let our matters pass!
How darest thou, dawcock, mell?
How darest thou, losél,
Allegate the Gospel
Against us of the council?
Avaunt to the devil of hell!
Take him, Warden of the Fleet,
Set him fast by the feet!
I say, Lieutenant of the Tower,
Make this lurdain for to lour;
Lodge him in Little Ease,
Feed him with beans and peas!
The King's Bench or Marshalsea,
Have him thither by and by!
The villain preacheth openly,
And declareth our villany;
And of our free simpleness,
He says that we are reckeless,
And full of wilfulness,
Shameless and merciless,
Incorrigible and insatiate;
And after this rate
Against us doth prate!

'At Paulès Cross or elsewhere,
Openly at Westminstere,
And Saint Mary Spittle,
They set not by us a whistle!
At the Austin Friars
They count us for liars!
And at Saint Thomas of Akers
They clack of us like crakers,
How we will rule all at will
Without good reason or skill;

And say how that we be
Full of partiality;
And how at a prong
We turn right into wrong,
Delay causes so long
That right no man can fong;
They say many matters be born
By the right of a ramès horn![1]
Is not this a shameful scorn,
To be tearéd thus and torn?

  'How may we this endure?
Wherefore we make you sure,
Ye preachers shall be yawed;
And some shall be sawed,
As noble Isaias,
The holy prophet, was;
And some of you shall die,
Like holy Jeremy;
Some hangéd, some slain,
Some beaten to the brain;
And we will rule and reign,
And our matters maintain,
Who dare say there again,[2]
Or who dare disdain,
At our pleasure and will.
For, be it good or be it ill,
As it is, it shall be still,—
For all master doctor of Civil,
Or of Dominic, or doctor Drivel,
Let him cough, rough, or snivel!
Run God, run Devil,
Run who may run best,
And let take all the rest!

[1] by justice as crooked as a ram's horns
[2] Whoever dare say anything against it

We set not a nutshell
The way to heaven or hell!'

    Lo, this is the guise nowadays!
It is to dread, men says,
Lest they be Sadducees,
As they be said sain,[1]
Which determinéd plain
We should not rise again
At dreadful doomèsday.
And so it seemeth they play,
Which hate to be corrected
When they be infected,
Nor will suffer this book
By hook ne by crook
Printed for to be,
For that no man should see
Nor read in any scrolls
Of their drunken nolls,
Nor of their nodipolls,
Nor of their silly souls,
Nor of some witless pates
Of divers great estates,
As well as other men.

    Now to withdraw my pen,
And now a while to rest,
Meseemeth it for the best.

    The forecastle of my ship
Shall glide, and smoothly slip
Out of the wavès wood
Of the stormy flood;
Shoot anchor, and lie at road,
And sail not far abroad,

[1] called commonly

Till the coast be clear,
And the lode-star appear.
My ship now will I steer
Toward the port salu
Of our Saviour Jesu,
Such grace that He us send,
To rectify and amend
Things that are amiss,
When that His pleasure is.
    Amen!

from The Garland of Laurel (1523)

By Saint Mary, my lady,
Your mammy and your daddy
Brought forth a goodly baby!

My maiden Isabel,
Reflaring rosabel.
The fragrant camomel;
The ruddy rosary,
The sovereign rosemary,
The pretty strawberry;
The columbine, the nept,
The jelofer well set,
The proper violet:
Ennewéd your colour
Is like the daisy flower
After the April shower;
Star of the morrow gray,
The blossom on the spray,
The freshest flower of May;
Maidenly demure,
Of womanhood the lure;
Wherefore I make you sure
It were an heavenly health,
It were an endless wealth,
A life for God himself,
To hear this nightingale
Among the birdès smale
Warbeling in the vale,
Dug, dug,
Jug, jug,
Good year and good luck,
With chuck, chuck, chuck, chuck!

To Mistress Margaret Hussey

Merry Margaret,
  As midsummer flower,
Gentle as falcon
Or hawk of the tower:
With solace and gladness,
Much mirth and no madness,
All good and no badness;
    So joyously,
    So maidenly,
    So womanly
    Her demeaning
    In every thing,
    Far, far passing
    That I can indite,
    Or suffice to write
Of Merry Margaret
  As midsummer flower,
Gentle as falcon
Or hawk of the tower.
  As patient and still
And as full of good will
As fair Isaphill,
Coriander,
Sweet pomander,
Good Cassander,
Steadfast of thought,
Well made, well wrought,
Far may be sought
Ere that ye can find
So courteous, so kind
As Merry Margaret,
  This midsummer flower,
Gentle as falcon
Or hawk of the tower.

from A Replication (1529)

King David the prophet, of prophetès principal,
    Of poetès chief poet, Saint Jerome doth write,
Resembléd to Simonides, that poet lyrical
    Among the Greeks most relucent of light,
     In that faculty which shinéd as Phoebus bright:
Like to Pindarus in glorious poetry,
Like unto Alcaeus, he doth him magnify.

Flaccus nor Catullus with him may not compare,
    Nor solemn Serenus, for all his harmony
In metrical muses, his harping we may spare;
    For David, our poet, harpéd so melodiously
     Of our Saviour Christ in his decachord psaltry,
That at his resurrection he harpéd out of hell
Old patriarchs and prophets in heaven with him to dwell.

        Then, if this noble king
        Thus can harp and sing
        With his harp of prophecy
        And spiritual poetry,
        As Saint Jerome saith,
        To whom we must give faith,
        Warbling with his strings
        Of such theological things,
        Why have ye then disdain
        At poetès, and complain
        How poets do but feign?

         Ye do much great outrage
        For to disparage
        And to discourage
        The fame matriculate
        Of poetès laureate.
         For if ye sadly look,

And wisely read the Book
Of Good Advertisement,
With me ye must consent
And infallibly agree
Of necessity,
How there is a spiritual,
And a mysterial,
And a mystical
Effect energial,
As Greekès do it call,
Of such an industry,
And such a pregnancy,
Of heavenly inspiration
In laureate creatíon,
Of poets commendation,
That of divine miseration
God maketh his habitation
In poetès which excels,
And sojourns with them and dwells.

By whose inflammation
Of spiritual instigation
And divine inspiration
We are kindled in such fashion
With heat of the Holy Ghost
(Which is God of mightès most),
That he our pen doth lead,
And maketh in us such speed
That forthwith we must need
With pen and ink proceed,
Sometime for affectíon,
Sometime for sad direction,
Sometime for correction,
Sometime under protection
Of patient sufferance,
With sober circumstance,

Our mindès to advance
To no man's annoyance;
Therefore no grievance,
I pray you, for to take
In this that I do make
Against these frenetics,
Against these lunatics,
Against these schismatics,
Against these heretics,
Now of late abjuréd,
Most unhappily uréd:
For be ye well-assuréd
That frenzy, nor jealously,
Nor heresy will never die.